PROFESSIONAL STUDIO TECHNIQUES

WEB DESIGN ESSENTIALS

SECOND EDITION

MARIA GIUDICE AND ANITA DENNIS

Web Design Essentials, Second Edition

Maria Giudice with Anita Dennis

Copyright © 2001 Adobe Press

This Adobe Press book is published by Peachpit Press.
For information on Adobe Press books, contact

Peachpit Press
1249 Eighth Street
Berkeley, CA 94710
510-524-2178 • 800-283-9444
510-524-2221 (fax)
http://www.peachpit.com

Peachpit Press is a division of Pearson Education

For the latest on Adobe Press books, go to
http://www.adobe.com/adobepress

ISBN 0-201-73356-0
9 8 7 6 5 4 3 2 1
Printed and bound in the United States of America

▲
Easy

▲
Intermediate

▲
Advanced

Web Design Essentials offers advice for all levels of designers. At the beginning of each technique is a guide that indicates whether it is easy, intermediate, or advanced. If you're a beginner, you can start with the easy lessons and work your way up to the more challenging ones.

Introduction

Today's Web designers face more challenges than ever.

So you want to design a Web site? Perhaps you want to put a small, unpretentious site together to promote your business. Maybe you dabble in Web design and want to improve your skills so that you can take on bigger and better clients. Or maybe you're one of many designers at a corporate site and you want to learn how to create more efficient, perhaps even interactive, pages.

Web Design Essentials, *Second Edition*, is for each of you. In fact, it's for anyone who wants to know how to use Adobe's various design applications to create streamlined, stylish Web pages and sites.

Inside this book you'll find an assortment of step-by-step techniques that can help you take full advantage of all that Adobe's software has to offer. All good software offers multiple ways of executing the same task; Adobe products are no exception. As the applications evolve and upgrade, their functionality increasingly overlaps. That can leave both new and experienced designers wondering which tasks should be performed in which applications.

There's no easy answer to that question, but we've put together what we think is the best advice from real-world designers on some of the most important design and production issues. The techniques on the following pages are personalized, tried-and-true methods that will not only make your everyday workflows easier but make your Web sites look good, too. Try them and you'll see. Then experiment and perhaps you'll find a different way to do the same thing that works even better for you.

We think these techniques will pay off in numerous important ways, both professionally and personally. You'll please clients by producing sites with fast-loading and well-placed graphics, cohesive color and typography across platforms and browsers, and a clear and consistent navigational interface. Plus, you'll have the satisfaction of successfully tackling the most exciting technological and design challenges to come along in decades.

Thankfully, Web software tools have matured to a point where they make our job a little easier.

Now that we've told you what this book has to offer, it's also important to share what it doesn't. This book *won't* teach you: how to design—what makes a good layout, how to compose color, and so on—and it's not a tutorial for the various applications we cover. Rather, *Web Design Essentials, Second Edition*, will teach you how to use Adobe's tools to implement your creative vision, accommodating the medium's limitations (limited color palette, for example, and lack of control over typography) and making the most of its strengths (support for interactivity and animation, for example).

So although no tool will make you a better designer, you can improve the way you implement the design through the tools themselves. And that's what *Web Design Essentials, Second Edition*, is all about: using the tools more effectively to create better designed Web sites.

Although *Web Design Essentials, Second Edition*, covers the current versions of Adobe software for both the Macintosh and Windows—including Photoshop 6.0, ImageReady 3.0, Illustrator 9.0, GoLive 5.0, and LiveMotion 1.0—you can accomplish many of these techniques on older versions of the same programs.

Finally, wherever possible, our instructions are written in platform-neutral language, but keyboard shortcuts are presented in red with the Macintosh key commands first followed by the Windows equivalent after a slash.

Acknowledgements

Web Design Essentials, Second Edition, was created thanks to the team at

We especially appreciate Renee Anderson's tireless and efficient project management, which kept us all on track and on time. Jenny Eng's contribution to the book was also critical: She spearheaded the design and production of pages.

We're also grateful to the following members of the HOT team: Gregory Ramsperger, Julia Hummelt, Susan E. Stanger, David Knupp, Laura Dorothy Haertling, Dohyun Kim, and Zanne deJanvier, for mastering the applications in this book, sharing their expert techniques, and creating the beautiful art that illustrates the concepts.

Finally, many thanks to Amy Franceschini for her cover artwork; to Nancy Ruenzel, Jill Marts Lodwig, and Victor Gavenda at Peachpit Press for their editorial guidance; to Christine Yarrow, Daniel Brown, Morty Golding, John Nack, and Paul Chavez at Adobe for their recommendations and review; and to Tema Goodwin and FireCrystal Communications for their editorial assistance.

Table of Contents

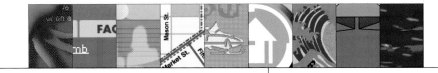

Creating Web Graphics

Chapter 1

Tiling a Background

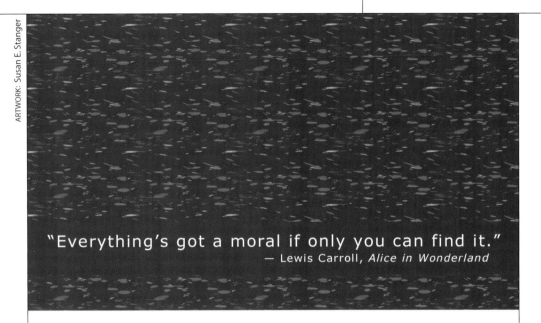

"Everything's got a moral if only you can find it."
— Lewis Carroll, *Alice in Wonderland*

One of the first tasks you'll have to tackle when designing a Web page is preparing a background. There are several techniques you can use. One is to create a single large background image and define "slices" that fit into the cells in an HTML table (see page 46). You can also create a basic, repetitive pattern using ImageReady's DitherBox feature (see page 16). But sometimes you don't want to construct HTML tables or worry about matching colors across sliced images. In those instances, or when you want to be more creative with your pattern than the DitherBox feature allows, ImageReady's Tile Maker filter comes in handy. The Tile Maker filter lets you create a background tile from an original image of, say, a muted pattern in Photoshop. Then visitors' browsers will repeat the tile automatically across the Web page.

1 Start by creating an image in Illustrator or Photoshop from which you'll marquee a tile. Here we experimented with Illustrator's Artistic brushes, drawing with the Paintbrush tool and applying different color strokes over a solid background layer. As you're designing, keep in mind that small patterns work best for tiled backgrounds, and try to work with a Web-safe palette.

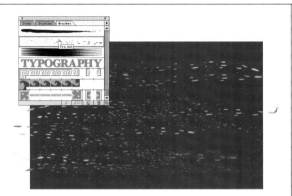

2 When you're satisfied with the pattern you've created, export the file as a 72-dpi RGB Photoshop file.

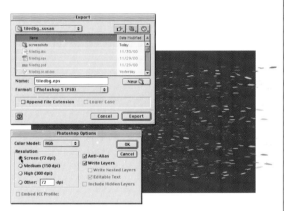

3 Open the image in ImageReady, and select an area that you want to use for your tile with the rectangular Marquee tool. You might have to experiment with size and position to select an area that creates a good pattern and yet is a small tile.

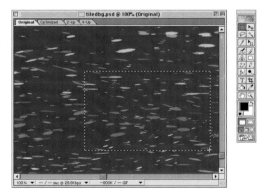

10

RELATED TIPS:

Expanding on the Web-safe Palette, page 16
Slicing Images for HTML Tables, page 46

4 Choose Tile Maker from the Filter menu (under Other). Select the Blend Edges option and specify a width. A percentage between 5 and 15 works best. Check Resize Tile so that the tile isn't reduced by the amount specified in Width. (The Kaleidoscope Tile option flips and duplicates the selection horizontally and vertically to create an abstract design.) Click OK.

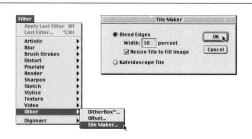

5 Choose Crop from the Image menu to reduce the file to the size of the tile. Click OK.

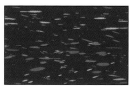

6 To preview your tile as a background in a browser, choose Output Settings from the File menu, and select Background. In the Output Settings dialog box, click the View As Background radio button, then click OK.

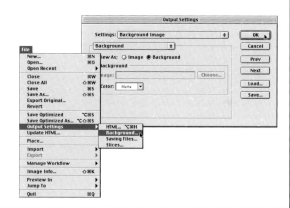

7 Choose Preview In from the File menu and choose your preferred browser.

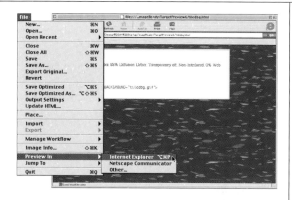

8 Optimize your tile as a GIF in the Save for Web dialog box. If your tile contains transparency, select the Transparency check box and apply a matte that matches your HTML page background (see page 25 for more on background transparency). Then choose File > Save Optimized As, and save your tile in the folder that contains your other Web site images. Select HTML and Images as your Format so that you can import the code and the tile into GoLive.

9 To place your tile on a page in GoLive, click the Page icon in the document window to access the Page Inspector. In the Background section, check the Image box and browse to select your tile.

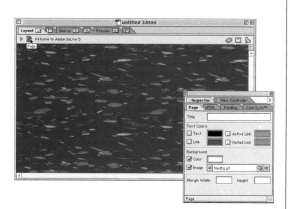

Selecting and Replacing Colors

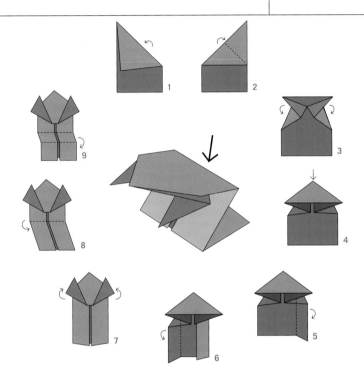

Creating Web graphics in RGB mode is the ideal, but in reality designers frequently prepare materials for the Web that were originally designed for print. This means converting files that were saved as CMYK into RGB mode. Sounds like an easy task—just choose RGB mode from Photoshop's Image menu, right? But it's not that straightforward. Certain CMYK values that might have been chosen deliberately to print well may not look good in RGB. And when you optimize your GIF file and reduce the number of colors in the image, the colors may shift even more, potentially destroying the integrity of the image. The ability to control the colors in image files by choosing specific pixels and replacing them at your discretion is an essential skill for effective Web design.

1 Open the CMYK document in Photoshop and change the mode by choosing Mode > RGB Color from the Image menu.

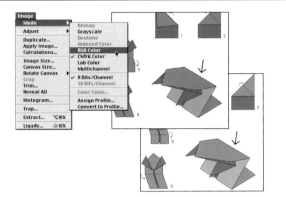

2 To get a feel for how your image quality will deteriorate if displayed in Web-safe colors (the worst-case scenario), choose Save for Web from the File menu. Choose GIF as your file format and apply the Web color reduction algorithm. Notice that some of the colors have dithered and shifted. Click Cancel to go back to the main document.

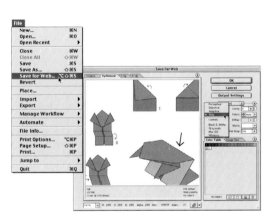

3 Use the Magic Wand to select the first color that needs to be replaced. On the tool options bar, designate a low Tolerance, but be prepared to increase this value if the tool doesn't capture the right pixels. Then check Anti-aliased if you want soft edges for the selection; Contiguous if you want to select only adjacent pixels; or Use All Layers if you want to capture pixels on layers other than the one that's active.

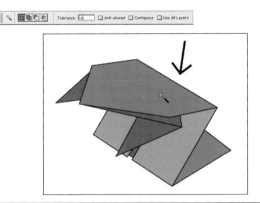

RELATED TIPS:
Dithering Part of an Image, page 14
Understanding Color Palettes, page 104

4 Click on the foreground color swatch to access the Color Picker, and then check the Only Web Colors box. Move the mouse over the image and use the Eyedropper to pick up the color from the image. The Color Picker converts it to the closest Web-safe color.

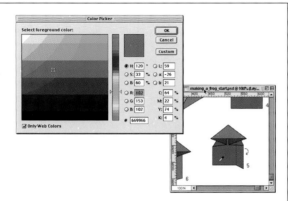

5 Choose Fill from the Edit menu and check Foreground Color in the Contents box. If you apply a blending mode, be aware that you will add non-Web-safe colors to the file.

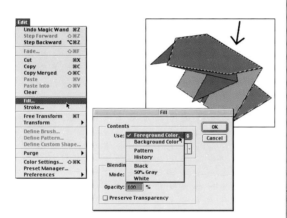

6 Repeat Steps 3, 4, and 5 until all the colors that shifted dramatically in the CMYK-to-RGB conversion are replaced.

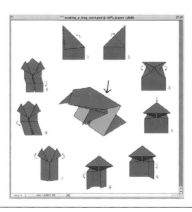

7 To make sure the colors you've so painstakingly chosen aren't eliminated when you optimize the GIF file, lock them in place. First, choose File > Save for Web and view the image in the Original tab of the Save for Web dialog box. Then press Shift and click on each replaced color with the Eyedropper tool. They'll be highlighted in the Color Table. Finally, click the Lock button at the bottom of the table to preserve these colors in the image.

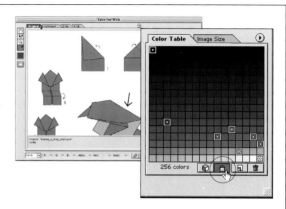

8 Optimize your graphic by selecting the appropriate color reduction algorithm, number of colors, dithering setting, and so on. Notice that all of the locked colors remain intact.

Using Select Color Range

Here's another way to capture all the pixels of a given color—especially if they're dispersed throughout the image and are hard to see. First choose Color Range from the Select menu, then choose Sampled Colors from the pop-up menu and click the desired area with the Eyedropper. Adjust the Fuzziness slider until you've included the appropriate pixels in your selection; click OK when you're satisfied. Then replace the selected pixels with a new foreground color by pressing Option-Delete/Alt-Backspace.

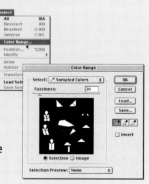

Dithering Part of an Image

Dithering is the computer-generated substitution of color, which occurs on a browser when a visitor's 256-color monitor displays an image composed of colors beyond its limited palette. This kind of dithering causes colors to shift, potentially compromising the integrity of the image. However, designers can combat this effect by deliberately dithering a GIF image when saving it for the Web, so that adjacent pixels simulate an intermediate color value, and thus create more subtle, pleasing color variations. But don't get carried away— dithering also bloats file size. An even better alternative is channel-based dithering, a feature in Photoshop 6.0 and ImageReady 3.0 that lets you apply dithering selectively, so that you have greater control not only over the final appearance of your image, but over the file size as well. Here we show you how.

1 Open your image in Photoshop and choose Save for Web from the File menu. Click the 4-Up tab so that you can view multiple optimized variations of your image at the same time.

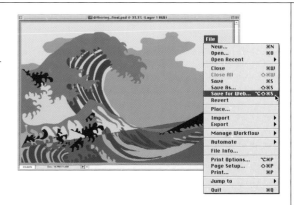

2 Study the various optimized versions of the image and decide how much you want to trade off image quality for small file size. In this example, applying 16 Web-safe colors drastically changes the original image; in particular, some of the water turns an unsuitable green (see lower-left corner). Adding a 100% dither brings the hue back into the blue spectrum, but it also creates a distracting interference pattern (lower-right corner).

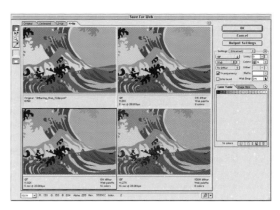

3 Since a straightforward dither doesn't give us the control we want over the green hue, we'll go back to the original image (click Cancel) and create an alpha channel for the green water. Then we'll go back to the Save for Web dialog box and dither just that channel.

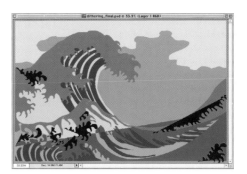

14

4 Select the Magic Wand and on the tool options bar, uncheck the Contiguous and Anti-aliased boxes. Then click on the "green" water to cleanly select all of the desired pixels.

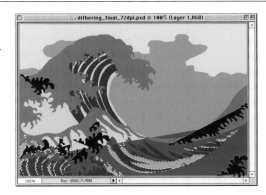

5 Click the Save selection as channel button at the bottom of the Channels palette. Rename this new channel, Alpha 1, something more intuitive by double-clicking it. Enter the new name in the Channel Options dialog box, and choose Color Indicates: Masked Areas. Click OK. Then back on the Channels palette, click the eye icon for the RGB composite channel to view the mask in the image.

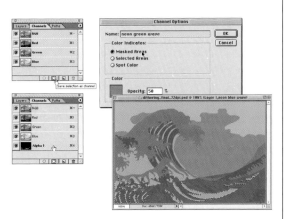

6 Choose Save for Web from the File menu again, this time using the 2-Up view so that you can see the original and the optimized images. Choose Web as your color reduction algorithm and reduce the number of colors to as few as possible.

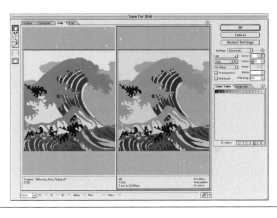

7 Now choose Diffusion as your dither method, and click the Modify Dither Settings button next to the Dither text box. In the Modify Dither Settings dialog box, select your green-wave channel from the pull-down menu and either play with the sliders or enter percentages in the text boxes to specify the amount of dithering you want.

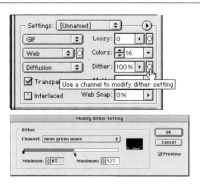

8 Keep the Preview box checked so that you can see the results in the 2-Up view window. When you're satisfied, click OK.

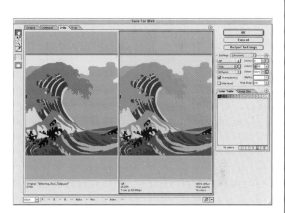

9 Because you can't dither multiple alpha channels in the same GIF, you need to select all the areas you want dithered in one alpha channel, or combine separate alpha channels into one before saving for the Web. (See page 110 for help with creating and combining alpha channels.)

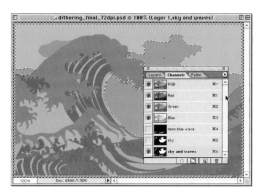

Expanding on the Web-safe Palette

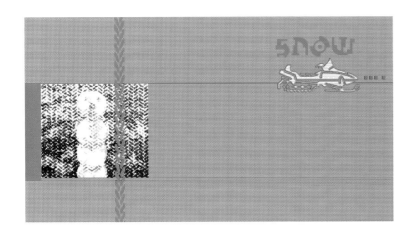

The palette of 216 Web-safe colors is harsh and restrictive, with saturated hues that are too garish to use in many backgrounds and graphics, particularly for corporate sites. To make matters worse, corporate Web sites often require colors that aren't even part of the Web-safe palette. Fortunately, you can create the appearance of soft, unique, browser-safe colors using Photoshop and ImageReady's DitherBox feature. DitherBox simulates any color using Web-safe alternatives, giving you more control over your site's appearance and minimizing the potential for unappealing browser dither. Here we provide an overview of how to use this feature.

1 Start with a new Photoshop image and fill it with the color you want on your Web page, such as the blue shown here. Click the foreground color swatch on the toolbar and choose a hue in the Color Picker. Select Fill from the Edit menu, and choose Foreground Color for Contents.

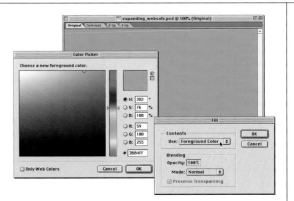

2 Choose Other from the Filter menu, and then choose DitherBox. The filter applies a 2-x-2-pixel default dither pattern with a second color. If you've used DitherBox before, it will display your previous pattern. To clear it and create a new one, click the RBG-to-Pattern arrow to replace the old pattern with one based on the currently selected color.

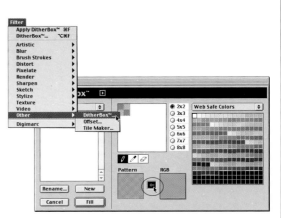

3 To change a pixel in the dither pattern grid, select a new color on the Web Safe Colors palette, and with the Pencil tool click the appropriate pixel in the dither pattern grid. To delete a color, use the Eraser tool and click in the grid.

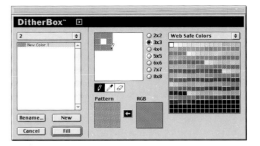

RELATED TIPS:
Dithering Part of an Image, page 14

Adobe Photoshop 6.0   Adobe ImageReady 3.0   Adobe GoLive 5.0

4 The Pattern box shows a preview of each edit that you make. When you're satisfied, click Fill, and then view the pattern applied to the full background image.

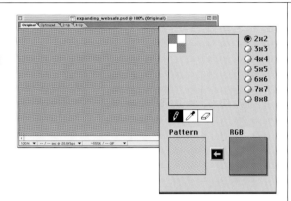

7 To apply the tile to an HTML page background, click the Page icon in a document window in GoLive to access the Page Inspector. Check the Image box in the Background section and browse to select your tile file.

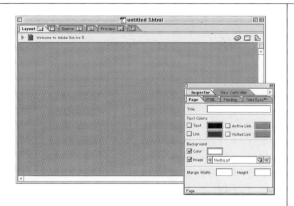

5 Alternatively, you can save the pattern so that you can apply it to other files. To do so, first edit the pattern in the DitherBox until you are satisfied and then click Cancel. Photoshop or ImageReady will ask whether you want to save the new pattern. Click OK.

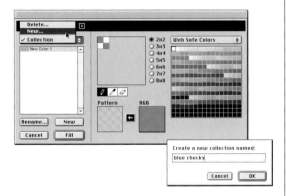

8 You can make the Ditherbox pattern grid as large as 8-x-8 pixels, with several colors and any creative pattern. As you experiment, keep in mind that similar hues work best, especially if you want the pattern to be subtle. To make a color seem less saturated, use white as one of your colors.

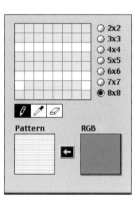

6 Then create a new image with the same dimensions as the DitherBox pattern you created in Step 5— 2-x-2 pixels in our example. Open the DitherBox as in Step 2, select the pattern, and click Fill.

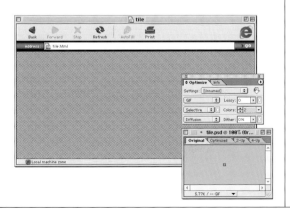

9 You can also apply the DitherBox filter to a selected area of an image: use any of the selection marquee tools, or make a specific layer of the image visible on the Layers palette, and apply the dither to just that area or layer.

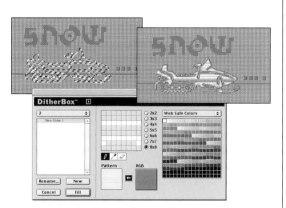

It's not uncommon for several designers in an office to be working on different pages of the same Web site at once. As the project progresses, the site expands and pages become more complex. Then it quickly becomes difficult to keep track of changes made to visual elements such as navigational graphics and corporate logos, and to make sure everyone is using the most current versions of files. If you are the lucky soul responsible for creating and sharing the buttons, for example, you'll have to track how you created a certain style of button and explain the steps to your peers. Using Layer Styles is a great way to manage this situation. After you have finessed the effects on one button, you can simply save the steps as a style and then apply it to other buttons, or you can pass the layer style to co-workers so that they can apply it to the buttons on their pages, too.

1 If you've created the basic button icons in Illustrator, as we have in this example, export them in Photoshop (PSD) format. This preserves the layers you've created when you open and work on the files in Photoshop.

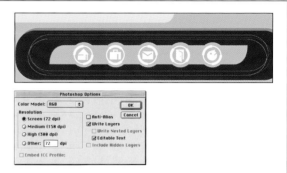

2 Open your button image file in Photoshop. To prepare the buttons for an effect, first create a new layer by clicking the Create New Layer button at the bottom of the Layers palette, or by choosing New Layer from the palette's pop-up menu. Position the new layer under the first button layer—Home, in this example—and use the Layer Properties command in the Layer menu to name it. We've labelled ours "Back circle"; you'll see why in a moment.

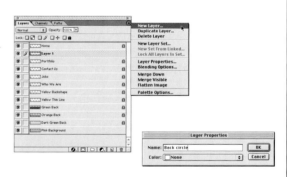

3 Since Photoshop automatically fills the shape you are about to draw with the foreground color, you might want to choose a color that you want to be part of your layer effect first. Then on this layer, use one of the vector tools to trace the first button: We used the Ellipse tool and pressed Shift while dragging to draw a circle.

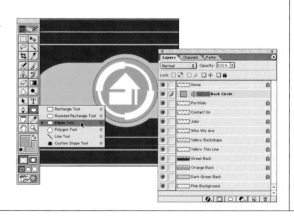

18

RELATED TIPS:
Enhancing Type with Layer Effects, page 40
Animation Styles, page 74
Using Layer Sets to Manage Files, page 98

Adobe Illustrator 9.0   Adobe Photoshop 6.0

4 Copy the shape layer by selecting Duplicate Layer from the Layer menu or from the Layers palette pop-up menu, and position the duplicate under the layer for the second button icon. Repeat this process until you have a copy of the shape layer under each button layer. Now apply an effect to the original shape layer. Double-click on the layer name to display the Layer Style dialog box.

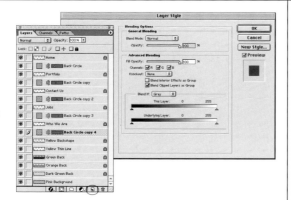

5 To create the effect, we first applied a Drop Shadow, setting the Blend Mode to Overlay. We used the default settings for everything else, including color (black), opacity (75 percent), and angle (30 degrees).

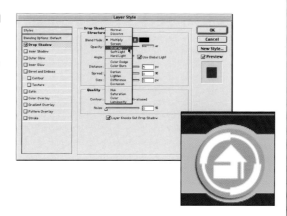

6 We also applied Bevel & Emboss, specifying an Inner Bevel as the Style, a Highlight Mode of Overlay, and a Shadow Mode of Multiply. That way, the colors in the original button layer are mixed with the effect colors, preserving the lightness and darkness of the original. When you are satisfied, click OK.

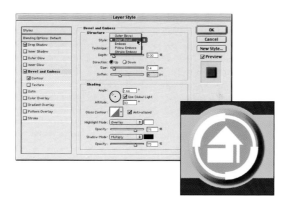

7 Now you can save your effects as a style. To do this, make sure the layer you have been working on is active (in this case "Back circle"), and then select New Style from the Styles palette's pop-up menu. (Alternatively, you can click on the New Style button before you exit the Layer Style dialog box.)

8 Give your style a concise and descriptive name such as "Bevel & Shadow Button," and include layer effects and blending options. Now you can apply your effect to other shape layers with a click of the mouse. On the Layers palette, select the first duplicated shape you created in Step 4 ("Back Circle copy" in this example) and then click the style you just created on the Styles palette ("Bevel & Shadow" here).

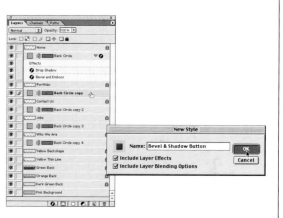

9 Repeat the process for the rest of the duplicate shape layers until you've applied the effect to all the navigational buttons in the file.

Creating Web Graphics   **19**

Mapping Made Easy

ARTWORK: David Knupp & Zanne deJanvier/Hot Studio, Inc.

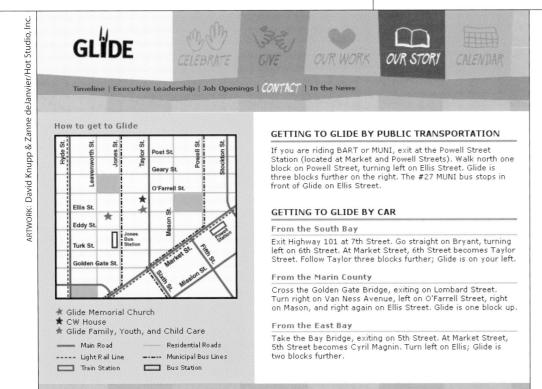

It may be mundane, but one of the most common reasons visitors check out a Web site is to glean contact information about a particular company or organization—to get a snail mail address, for example, or to find directions to an organization's headquarters. For Web designers whose forte isn't cartography, drawing maps might be intimidating. But thanks to Illustrator 9.0's graphic styles, it's easy to draw simple maps. The graphic styles can be applied to layers, letting you maintain consistency across an illustration or an entire site. Here's how we used them to create a map for Glide Memorial United Methodist Church in San Francisco.

1 Create a new document in RGB mode and use the Rectangle tool to draw the background of your map. Fill the shape with an appropriate color (such as the light yellow in this example) by clicking on a hue on the Color palette. Then double-click the layer on the Layers palette to open the Layer Options dialog box, and then give the layer a descriptive name.

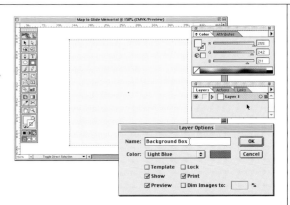

2 Now prepare the border outline of the map. First choose Duplicate from the Layers palette pop-up menu and None from the Color palette to remove the fill. Then apply a heavy black stroke, perhaps 3 points. Name this layer by double-clicking it on the Layers palette, which opens the Layer Options dialog box. Throughout this exercise, this layer and the background layer you created in Step 1 should remain the top layer and bottom layer, respectively.

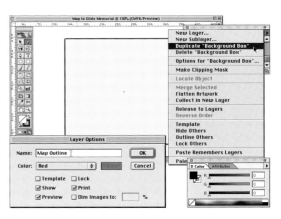

3 Select the background layer on the Layers palette and click the Create New Layer button at the bottom of the the Layers palette. This layer will contain the map's main thoroughfares. Draw the first road using the Pen tool, applying an appropriate color (brown, for example) and weight (3 points, the same weight as in step 2).

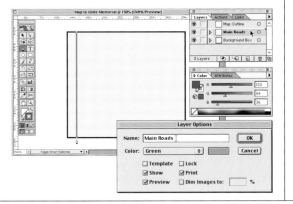

RELATED TIPS:

Managing Page Elements with Layer Styles, page 18
Animation Styles, page 74

4 Now create a style that you can apply to the other main roads in this layer. First, drag the Object icon that defines your road attributes from the Appearance palette to the Styles palette. Then double-click on it to give it a descriptive name.

5 Apply this style to the main thoroughfares layer by clicking the target icon on the Layers palette and then clicking the Main Roads style on the Styles palette. The target icon will fill to indicate that a style has been targeted. When you draw additional roads on this layer, they will automatically take on the appropriate attributes.

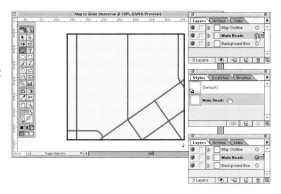

6 Now you can create additional layers for secondary roads, parks, and various modes of public transportation, and apply individual styles to each layer. Applying graphic styles helps you navigate more easily within the document and ensures that the appropriate style will always be applied to each layer as you draw.

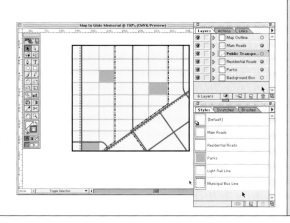

7 Label the roads using the Text tool on a separate layer, and add landmarks, such as bus and train stations, on another layer, creating styles for them, as well.

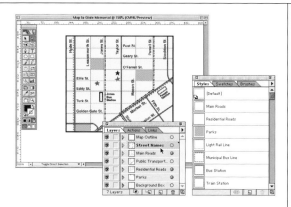

8 Finally, create a new layer and draw the legend using the styles you have created and saved on the Styles palette to quickly paint the symbols. When you're done, choose Save for Web from the File menu and optimize the map as a GIF with as few colors as possible.

Previewing Rasterized Graphics

Vector artwork created for the Web in Illustrator is ultimately saved as a pixel-based image.

To see how your vector graphic will look as a bitmapped image in a browser, zoom in and choose Pixel Preview from the View menu. See how jagged smooth curves become when they're anti-aliased? Pixel Preview snaps objects to a pixel grid, making it easy to see if lines are misplaced or become blurry when they're rasterized. Because Illustrator draws strokes down the center of paths, you may want to run a 0.5 pixel offset around 1-pixel strokes so that the path will have smooth edges: Choose Object > Path > Offset Path, and enter 0.5 pixels for the Offset amount.

Creating Artwork with Transparency

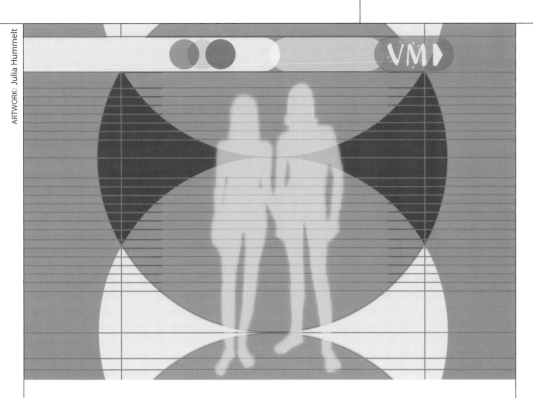

Transparency has been a four-letter word among digital artists who have long worked around Illustrator's limitations in this area. Previously we had to simulate varying degrees of opacity in Illustrator by choosing specific colors or gradients to create fades, soft shadows, and ghosting. Unfortunately, these techniques almost always left images looking flat and hard-edged. At last, however, we can now apply transparency to layers and objects using blending modes, saving us from switching to Photoshop to create realistic shadows and other transparent effects. Here's how to use Illustrator 9.0's transparency features when creating digital artwork; to learn how to apply background transparency to a Web graphic, see page 25.

1 To demonstrate how transparency works in Illustrator, we created a multilayered file, placing each type of object—ovals, lines, two colors of circles, text, and the background—on separate layers.

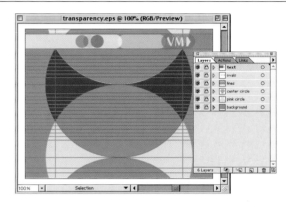

2 To specify the opacity and blending mode of a layer, select the layer on the Layers palette by clicking at the far right of the layer name, and then view the Transparency palette. (Or select the object or group of objects in the image and look at the palette.) Enter an opacity or click on the arrow next to the Opacity field to adjust the opacity using a slider; to change the blending mode from the default (Normal), use the pop-up menu.

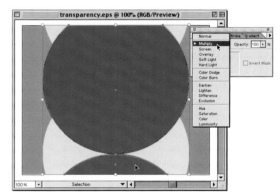

3 By changing the blending mode of our center blue circles to Multiply, for example, the pink circles and the red background in the layers below show through. Specifying an opacity of 50% makes the effect more subtle.

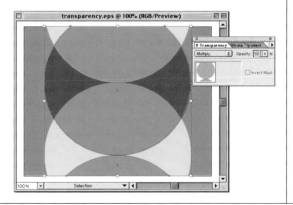

RELATED TIPS:
Mapping Made Easy, page 20
Understanding Blending Modes, page 106

4 Illustrator by default applies transparency effects to an object's fill and stroke, but you can apply transparency to one or the other. Select the object in the image window, or click the target icon for the object on the Layers palette, and view its stroke and fill characteristics, including transparency, on the Appearance palette. Here, we see a close-up view of the stroke of the blue circle, which is set at an opacity of 50%.

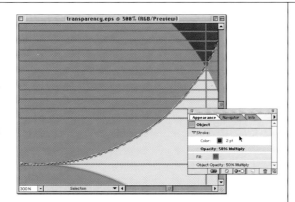

5 To change the transparency of the object's stroke, for example, select it on the Appearance palette and change the settings on the Transparency palette. Here, for example, we changed Multiply at 50% to Overlay at 100%.

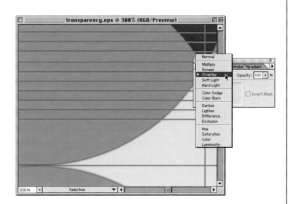

6 Now we will create an opacity mask, which lets underlying objects show through the objects or shapes above it. If the shape or object you want to use for the mask is part of your file, make sure the masking shape is at the front of your artwork (select it and choose Arrange > Bring to Front from the Object menu), and choose Make Opacity Mask from the Transparency palette pop-up menu.

7 In our example, however, we want to create a mask from a shape in another file—a bitmapped silhouette of two women, which contrasts with the rigid geometry of the art elements. First we create a new layer for that file by clicking the Create New Layer button at the bottom of the Layers palette, naming it, and placing that layer at the top of the stack.

8 Then draw a rectangle approximately the same size of the image that is to be placed, and fill it with any color (orange, in this case). We will cut out the mask from this shape.

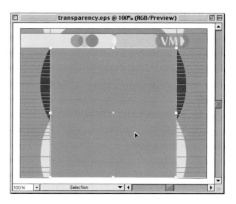

9 With your new layer selected, choose Place from the File menu. The placed image appears over the rectangle.

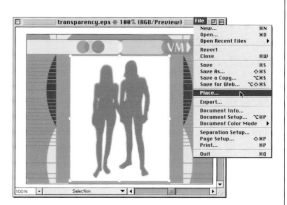

10 With both the placed image and the rectangle selected on the Layers palette, choose Arrange > Bring to Front from the Object menu, and then choose Make Opacity Mask from the Transparency palette pop-up menu.

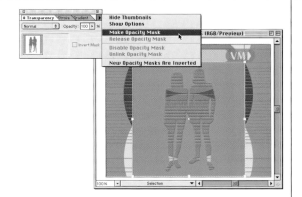

11 Check the Invert Mask box on the Transparency palette.

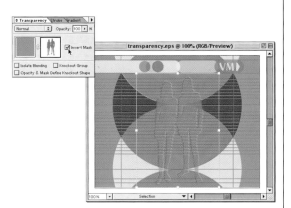

12 With the mask selected on the Layers palette and the left thumbnail selected on the Transparency palette, you can change the color of the masked shape by adjusting the RGB sliders on the Color palette.

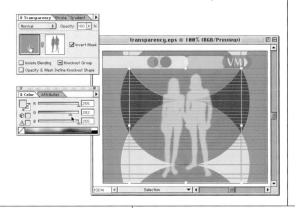

13 You can also add a blending mode, in this case Screen, and specify an opacity (100%) on the Transparency palette.

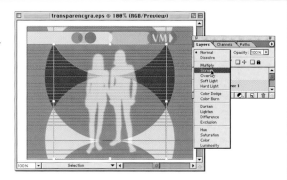

14 If your illustration needs further work or compositing with another piece of art in Photoshop, choose Export from the File menu and choose the Photoshop 5 (PSD) format. This preserves all transparent effects and retains the layers you created in Illustrator—except for nested layers, which are flattened into one layer.

15 In Photoshop, you can edit your artwork in a bitmapped environment, applying filters or layer effects (see page 18), for example, before choosing Save for Web.

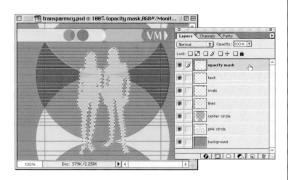

RELATED TIPS:

Mapping Made Easy, page 20
Understanding Blending Modes, page 106

16 If you export your artwork to another program that doesn't support transparency (such as Flash), you must flatten it first. With the Selection tool, select the objects you want to flatten (or use Command-A/Ctrl-A to select all) and choose Flatten Transparency from the Object menu. Your Rasterization Resolution should be 72 dpi for Web publishing.

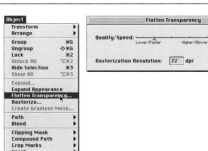

17 If you're satisfied with your art as you've created it in Illustrator and you're ready to import it into an HTML authoring program, choose Save for Web from the File menu.

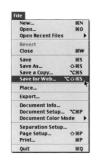

18 Choose an appropriate file format—usually GIF for artwork created in Illustrator, since you're working with vector graphics. We applied an Adaptive color reduction algorithm and saved with 64 colors. Since you don't want the HTML background to show through, do not check the Transparency box.

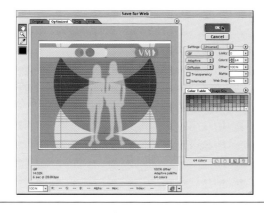

Background Transparency in Web Graphics

When you optimize an image in Illustrator, Photoshop, or ImageReady, you sometimes have the option of applying transparency. This is because both GIF and PNG formats allow you to preserve transparent pixels in an image so that the image blends more seamlessly with the HTML page background. Appropriately, Adobe calls this "background transparency."

GIF and PNG-8 support one level of background transparency, so if you choose one of these formats and select Transparency, all fully transparent pixels are preserved. PNG-24, however, supports up to 256 levels of transparency in an image. With PNG-24, pixels that are partially opaque will blend with the HTML background or matte color (we'll get to mattes in a moment). Use PNG-8 and PNG-24 with caution, however, as browsers do not universally support these file formats. (Internet Explorer 5.0 on the Mac supports transparency in PNG-8 and PNG-24; Internet Explorer for Windows supports PNG-8 in versions 5.0 and above. Netscape Navigator 4.0 and below does not support PNG, period; Navigator 6.0 supports transparency in PNG-8 and PNG-24 on both platforms.)

Selecting a matte color when you optimize a transparent GIF or PNG file fills or blends transparent pixels with the chosen color. This is called background matting, and it works best when you know the solid HTML background color and choose a matte that matches. Choosing None creates a hard-edged transparency, in which pixels that are more than 50% transparent become fully transparent in the file, and pixels with 50% or less transparency become fully opaque. Hard-edged transparency is more suitable when the HTML background is a pattern because this type of transparency can cause jagged edges in the image.

JPEG doesn't support transparency but it does allow you to apply a background matte. If you have an image with transparency and save it for the Web as JPEG, apply a matte that matches the (solid) HTML background. Fully transparent pixels will be filled with the matte color and partially transparent pixels will be blended with it, so when the JPEG is placed on a Web page with the same color background, the image will blend in smoothly.

Drawing a Navigational System

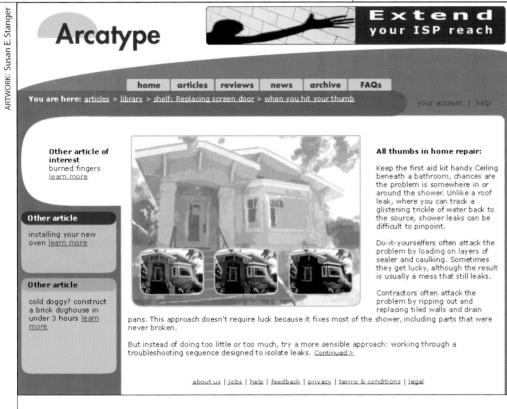

What happens when a client comes to you midway through a project wanting dramatic changes to the navigational system? In the past, you would probably have had to copy and paste existing tabs and buttons to accommodate the new links in your Photoshop comp, and then go through a cumbersome process of resizing everything to make a good fit. But Photoshop 6.0's vector tools make it easy to create and manage repetitive elements in your comp. Objects created with vector tools can easily be scaled down to make room for new additions—or scaled up to fill the void in case of deletions. As a bonus, if you import artwork from Illustrator, you can now edit those vector objects in Photoshop.

1 Choose one of Photoshop's vector tools and start drawing the first button or tab for your navigational system. Photoshop handles vector graphics on individual layers—just like it handles text—so it automatically places the shape on a new layer. To draw more shapes, choose New Layer from the Layers palette pop-up menu or from the Layer menu itself, name the layer in the New Layer dialog box, and draw.

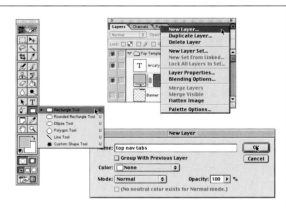

2 Because the shape will fill with the foreground color, first select your desired color in the Color Picker (orange, in our example). Then on the tool options bar, click the Create New Shape Layer button (as opposed to creating a new work path or a filled region) and specify your tool's Geometry Options by clicking the downward arrow. In our example, we're using a rounded rectangle with a 2-pixel radius.

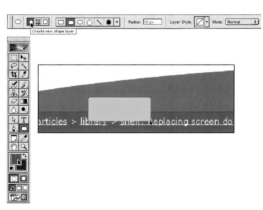

3 Edit your button until it is the desired shape. You can add or subtract nodes with the Add or Delete Anchor Point tools, and you can use the Convert Point tool to change the direction of lines. Use the Path Component Selection tool to modify path areas and to position the shape in the image. You can also use the pathfinder buttons on the options bar (add, subtract, intersect, and exclude) to create complex shapes.

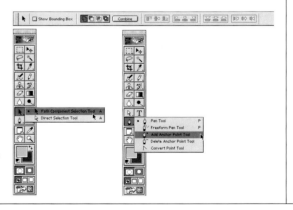

RELATED TIPS:

Transforming Type Using Vectors, page 36
Slicing Images for HTML Tables, page 46

4 To enhance the shape, apply a layer style as you draw. Click the downward arrow next to the Layer Style button on the options bar and choose from the styles in the picker. To change the fill of the shape after you've applied a particular color, gradient, or pattern, choose Change Layer Content from the Layer menu and select what you want to change. The Solid Color option, for example, lets you specify a new hue from the Color Picker.

5 When you're satisfied with the shape of your button or tab, simply copy and paste to create all the additional shapes you need. Choose the Direct Selection tool and press Shift-Option/Alt to maintain alignment, and then drag to create a duplicate shape in the desired location. Repeat this process until you've created all the shapes you need. Note that all of the shapes you've created remain on the same layer as the original.

6 Now it's time to label the navigational elements. With the button layer active, select the Type tool, choose a font and other specs on the options bar; click the first shape; and type. When you're done, click the Commit Transform button on the options bar. Repeat until you've named all the tabs. Link the text layers to the button vector layer so that if you need to reposition the buttons, the text will move with them.

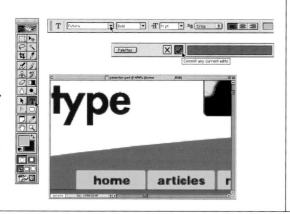

7 If your client requests different navigational links after you've completed the comp, it's easy to scale the tabs you've made and add more, because they're vector shapes. First, make the button shape layer active by unlinking the button and text layers. Then toggle off their visibility on the Layers palette.

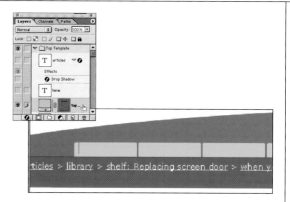

8 Using the Direct Selection tool, Shift-click to select all but one of the buttons, and press Delete. Scale the remaining button smaller by choosing the Edit > Transform > Scale path, and dragging to resize it. When you're done, press Return/Enter. Then press Shift-Option/Alt while dragging to create and position the appropriate number of duplicates as we did in Step 5.

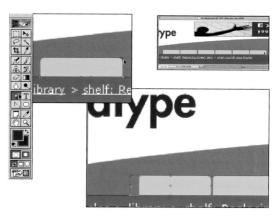

9 Finally, finetune the text labels. First make them visible and, one at a time, click on the word to enter Edit mode, reposition the cursor until it shows the Move tool icon, and drag to reposition the word back over the button. With the text selected, you can reduce the point size as necessary, or scale the text smaller after choosing Layer > Type > Convert to Shape and using the Transform command as described in the previous step.

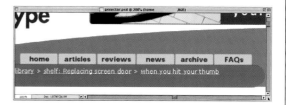

Creating Flexible Drop Shadows

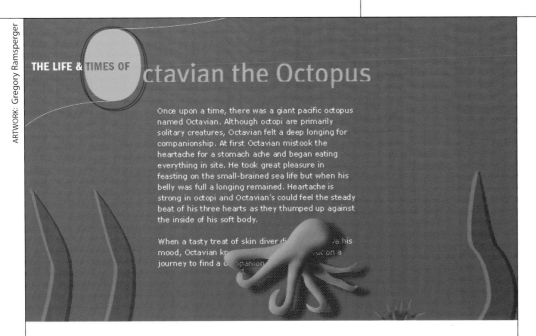

A drop shadow is a fundamental design element that enhances the appearance of graphics in print and on the Web, making them look anchored and stylish. Photoshop makes drop shadows easy to create with a Layer Style command, but that's actually a very fixed, limited approach. We prefer to create drop shadows as patterns that reside on their own layers. That way, you can reuse the shadow for multiple graphics and projects, and you can also customize it—distorting it, for example, to add a perspective—to suit your taste. And unlike Photoshop's Layer Style drop shadow, flexible shadows include transparent pixels, which let them blend seamlessly with HTML page background. Our approach also comes in handy if you plan to animate the object and its shadow later with DHTML—to learn how to do that, see page 76.

1 Using Photoshop, create a new 2-x-2-pixel, 72-dpi image in RGB mode with transparent contents. Then using the Pencil tool, with a 1-pixel brush, draw a single black pixel in the top-left corner of your image and another in the bottom-right corner. (You'll need to zoom way in to do this.)

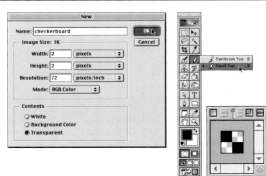

2 Press Command-A/Ctrl-A to select all, and then choose Define Pattern from the Edit menu. Name the pattern and click OK. You don't need to save the document; you've just created a preset pattern that can be used to fill a selection at any time in any Photoshop document. We'll use it now for our drop shadow.

 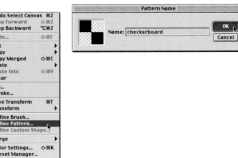

3 Open the image you want shadowed, making sure that the background and the object are on separate layers. Because the shape of the shadow will be based on the object, make sure the layer you want copied is selected, and then choose Duplicate Layer from the Layers palette pop-up menu.

RELATED TIPS:
Expanding on the Web-Safe Palette, page 16
Animating with DHTML, page 76

4   To soften the edges of the shadow's shape, blur the duplicate object. Choose Blur > Gaussian Blur from the Filter menu and keep the blur radius rather small, about 3 pixels. The new, blurred shape will be used as a template for creating the partially transparent shadow.

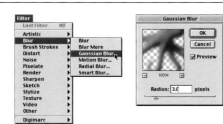

5   Create a new layer by clicking the Create New Layer button at the bottom of the Layers palette. Command-click/Ctrl-click on the blurred shape layer to select it.

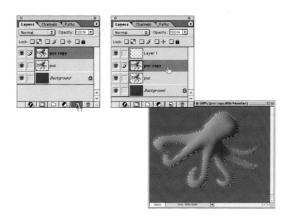

6   Choose Fill from the Edit menu. In the Fill dialog box, select Pattern from the Use pop-up menu, and then click the Custom Pattern box to access the Pattern Picker and choose your checkerboard pattern. Click OK to fill the selection with the pattern.

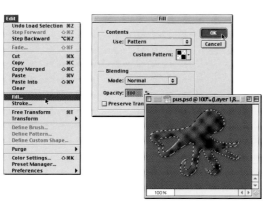

7   With the shadow layer active, use the Move tool to offset the shadow from the object. Move the shadow layer beneath the object layer on the Layers palette so that the object now appears on top of the shadow. Since you no longer need the blurry object, delete that layer by dragging it to the Trash can icon at the bottom of the Layers palette.

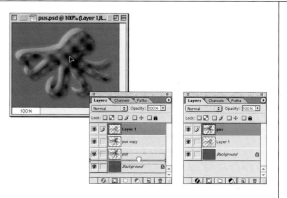

8   Turn off the background layer's visibility to make it transparent; that way the shadow will look correct when it's part of an HTML page. Choose Save for Web from the File menu and optimize the image as a GIF. Check the Transparency box and set a matte color that matches the background color of your HTML page. Specify your other optimization settings and click OK to save your image.

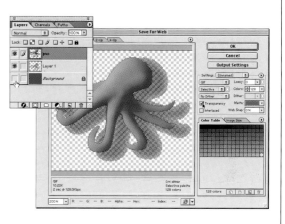

9   In an HTML page in GoLive, place your image in a floating box. If you use DHTML to animate the page, you will notice that the shadow appears semitransparent.

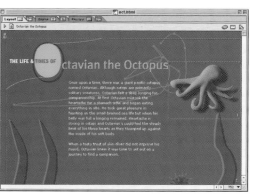

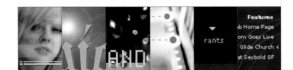

Managing Type | Chapter 2

Formatting Type for Comps

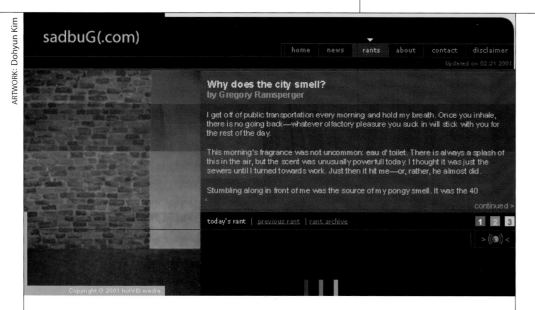

Not so long ago, designers cringed at the thought of editing large blocks of text in Photoshop because it had such cumbersome and awkward type tools: You had to toggle between the image itself and the text dialog box to edit the text, and the type controls (such as kerning and line spacing) were extremely limited. But when you prepare comps of Web pages for clients, working with type in Photoshop is a necessary evil—they need to see the type in the context of the page, even if ultimately the type that appears in the browser will be coded with HTML. Thankfully, Photoshop 6.0 boasts robust text-editing features much like those found in Illustrator, including character and paragraph formatting and the capability to type text directly onto an image. Here's how to manipulate type and simulate HTML text in your Photoshop Web page comp.

1 Create the background template for your Web page and then select the Type tool and position it over the image window. It changes to an I-beam cursor with a small line at the bottom indicating the base-line; click where you want to place text, and type a word or two. You have just set what Adobe calls "point type," an independent line of type that grows or shrinks as you edit it but doesn't wrap to the next line.

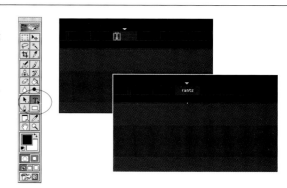

2 To format the text, select it by pressing Command-A/Ctrl-A or choosing All from the Select menu. In the options bar, you can specify a font family, font style, and point size. You can also specify anti-aliasing, alignment, and a color for your type. Remember that it's always preferable to use a Web-safe color to reduce the likelihood that the color will shift in a browser when a visitor sees it.

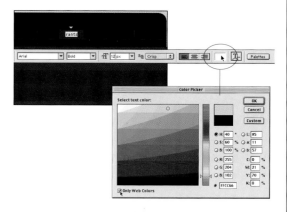

3 When you're satisfied, click OK (the button with the checkmark icon in the options bar) to commit the type to a layer. Then create additional lines of point type as desired by repeating Steps 1 and 2. Don't worry about precisely lining up your text; we'll do that next.

RELATED TIPS:
Previewing HTML Text in Comps, page 34
Enhancing Type with Layer Effects, page 40

4 In the Layers palette, you can see that Photoshop created a layer for each line of type that you entered. Select one of the text layers and then link it to the other text layers by clicking on the box between the layer visibility and the layer thumbnail icons. Go to the Layer menu, choose Align Linked, and align the lines along their bottom edges.

 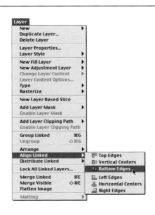

5 To let site visitors know they're actually on the Rants page, we will "dim" the names of the other two page links. Select the "In the News" layer on the Layers palette, and give the text a darker color by clicking the color swatch on the tool options bar. Select an appropriate color from the Color Picker that appears. Repeat for the "Final Thoughts" layer.

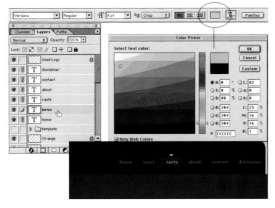

6 Now we'll add some secondary navigational text links. Select the Type tool and choose a font, color, and point size. Click where you want to position your text and type the first item. Without committing your changes, select a different color and type your other secondary navigational links. You have now created one text block containing multiple text formats.

7 Since the body of the page consists of a block of text, create a paragraph box. Using the Type tool, click and drag in the image to create a box for the text area. On the options bar, click the Palettes button to access the Character palette, where you can choose the formatting for the headline. Enter your headline, press Return/Enter, change the formatting, and type the subhead. Repeat for your body text, and then click Commit when you're done.

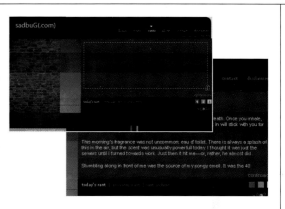

8 There are many other text formatting options available on the Character and Paragraph palettes. For instance, you can underline text so that it will look like a link, as we did here. If you're ambitious, you can also warp text using the button on the options bar, and apply Layer Styles to create glows, bevels, embosses, and more.

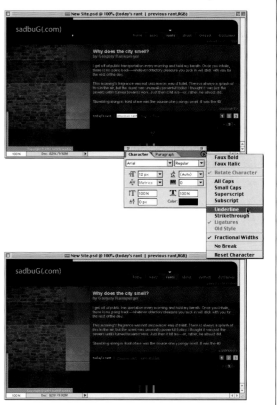

Previewing HTML Text in Comps

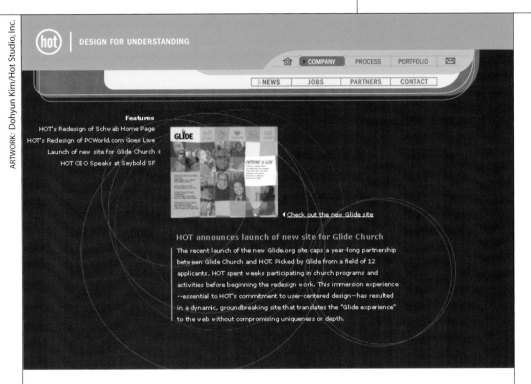

Working with text is one of the most challenging aspects of Web design. But the problem isn't just the fact that the designer doesn't have control over the appearance of type in the browser; it starts with the comp. If you lay out your comp in Illustrator, you need to know how to optimize the layers—especially those containing text—so that you can bring them into Photoshop and prepare an accurate pixel-based preview of HTML text for client approval. You also have to understand anti-aliasing, a technique that reduces the jaggy edges of letterforms and lines and smoothes the appearance of type or line art against its background. Here are a few tricks for managing HTML type as you prepare comps of Web pages.

1 When you create a Web page layout in Illustrator, you're working with anti-aliased text. Although both Windows 98/NT and Mac OS computers offer the option of smoothing fonts onscreen, you can't be sure if HTML text will look as smooth in a site visitor's browser, so it's important to export your comps to Photoshop for a more realistic preview for clients.

2 Since you know you'll be importing your Illustrator file into Photoshop, make sure the text layers in your design do not contain any graphical elements. If there is anything other than type on a text layer—any kind of path or shape—you will not be able to edit the text later in Photoshop.

3 When you're satisfied with your comp in Illustrator, make sure all the layers that you want to export are visible on the Layers palette, and then choose Export from the File menu.

34

RELATED TIPS:
Formatting Type for Comps, page 32
Using PDFs to Proof Comps, page 100

4 In the Export dialog box, select Photoshop 5 (PSD) from the Format pop-up menu and name your file. If you've previously saved your artwork as EPS or Illustrator, it's a good idea to choose a new name so that you don't accidentally overwrite the vector file with a bitmapped version. Then click Export.

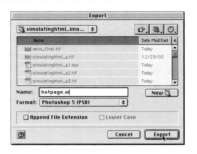

5 In the Photoshop Options dialog box that appears, select the RGB color model and 72-dpi resolution. Check the Write Layers box to preserve the individual layers of the file and check the Editable Text box so that you'll be able to edit the text in Photoshop. Check Anti-Alias to keep your artwork anti-aliased. Click OK.

6 When you open the file in Photoshop, a warning box tells you that some text layers might need to be updated before they can be used for vector-based output. Click the Update button. The layers that you created in Illustrator will appear on the Photoshop Layers palette; text layers are indicated by T.

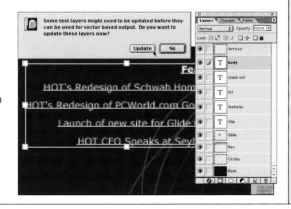

7 Select a layer that contains type that represents HTML text, choose the Type tool, and then select the text in the image. In the tool options bar, you'll see that the text is anti-aliased. Change the anti-aliased setting to None. Repeat for every layer containing type that represents HTML text.

8 By making all HTML text aliased, you'll give clients a better indication of how the text will appear in a browser window. Compare the aliased line of text at right (the headline and the top line of the paragraph) with the anti-aliased text (the remainder of the paragraph).

Designing Images with Type

You also have to wrestle with anti-aliasing when type is part of a bitmapped image, such as in a navigational button. When working with 9-point type or smaller, anti-aliasing may make the letters blurry and is not recommended. Also, be careful when using anti-aliased type over transparent graphics or patterned backgrounds, because the anti-aliasing might make the type harder to read. Finally, keep in mind that anti-aliasing adds color to a graphic file, so optimize final GIFs with enough colors to maintain the smoothing effect without bloating the file size.

Transforming Type Using Vectors

ARTWORK: Julia Hummelt

Until recently, designers had to turn to Illustrator for sophisticated type design because it offered more robust vector tools than Photoshop provided. Ultimately, however, you had to bring that artwork into your Photoshop Web page comp, which created an extra step in the process. Now, however, in addition to Photoshop 6.0's text-formatting options, the application can also treat type as vector shapes, which lets you skew, rotate, distort, and apply other transformations to your letters. Although Illustrator still has fancier vector brushes and effects and offers finer control over shapes, Photoshop's vector capabilities let you perform many basic transformations without having to switch applications, which makes the creative process that much easier. You simply convert your type layer to a shape and then manipulate as you would in Illustrator. But like Illustrator, Photoshop type treated as a vector object loses its editability, so you should always duplicate text layers before converting them to shapes.

1   Open your Photoshop document, select the type layer, and choose Type > Convert to Shape from the Layer menu.

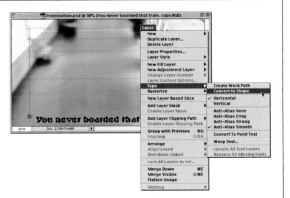

2   Using the Path Component Selection tool, select individual letters or Shift-click to select multiple letters. Make sure Show Bounding Box is checked on the tool options bar.

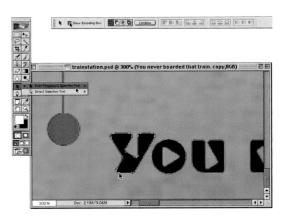

3   Simply drag on an edge or corner of the bounding box to change the letter's dimensions. This is called a "free transform." Press Shift to constrain the letter's proportions; press Command/Ctrl to freely stretch or skew the shape. Press Return/Enter to complete a transform.

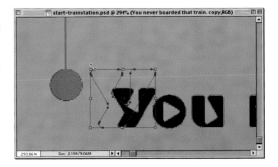

4 You can also use the Transform Path command in the Edit menu to apply such transforms as scale, rotate, skew, and distort. For example, here we chose Transform Path > Scale from the Edit menu, clicked on the bounding box, and then dragged to scale the shape.

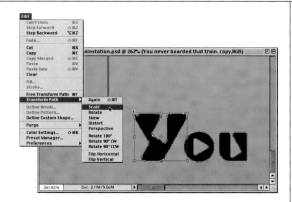

5 With the Direct Selection tool you can select and manipulate discrete path segments. Select the tool and click on a path anchor point, or drag across part of a letter to select part of a segment.

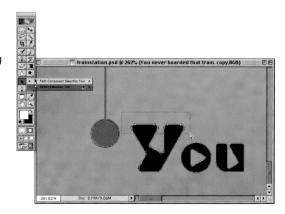

6 Change the shape by dragging the selected anchor points or segments, or move them by dragging from the center of the object or using the arrow keys on your keyboard.

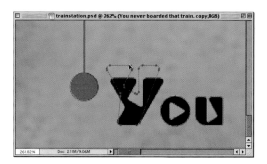

7 Continue selecting and editing components until you are satisfied.

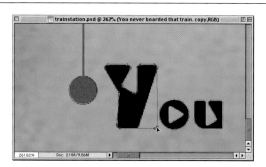

8 The Path Component Selection tool's options bar provides other vector operations, such as adding, subtracting, and intersecting shapes, as well as aligning and distributing them. Click the Combine button to combine all your letters into one shape so that you can edit them as a whole.

9 For example, we combined our letters and then chose Transform Path > Skew from the Edit menu to resize the text one last time.

Preserving Type in Bitmaps

Small file sizes are the name of the game in Web design, and although slicing an image is a common way to make large images appear to download quickly, that's not always the best option. Perhaps your client plans to maintain the site and doesn't want to manage all those files. Or perhaps the complex nature of the image makes it unsuitable for slicing. Luckily, Photoshop 6.0 and ImageReady 3.0 have a feature, called weighted optimization, that lets you optimize specific areas of an image based on alpha channels. This means you can apply separate color palettes, lossy compression settings, or dithering to discontiguous areas of GIF images, and separate quality settings to different areas of JPEGs. One of the best uses of weighted optimization, as we show here, is to preserve the legibility of text in a bitmapped image.

1 First make a mask of the area in your Photoshop image that you want to preserve. Flatten the image by choosing Flatten Image from the Layers palette pop-up menu, and then select the area using an appropriate tool. We used the Lasso tool to select the type.

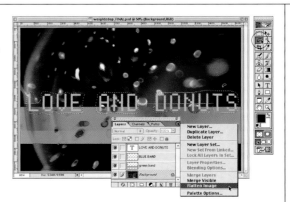

2 Click on the Save Selection as Channel button on the Channels palette to save your selection as a new alpha channel, Alpha 1. If you toggle on visibility Alpha 1 on the Channels palette, you'll see that the area you selected is white; all editing will affect that area of the image. The black area is protected from editing, or masked.

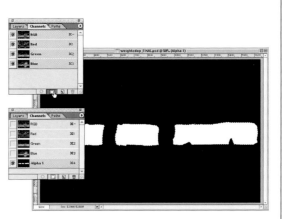

3 Choose Save for Web from the File menu; in the Save for Web dialog box specify your preferred file format. Our example is a photographic image, so we chose JPEG and applied a Medium (30) compression quality.

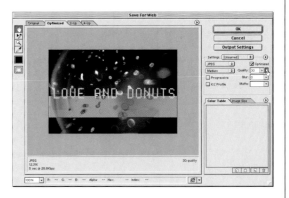

4 Notice the button with the small white circle next to the Quality text box. Click it to access the Modify Quality Setting dialog box.

5 Choose your channel mask (Alpha 1 for us) from the Channel pop-up menu and use the sliders to customize the quality for this channel. The Maximum (white) slider affects the optimization of the masked area—whose quality we want to preserve—so we leave it at a higher setting. The Minimum (black) slider affects the optimization of the rest of the image, so we will lower the quality here.

6 You might have to experiment to see what looks best for the image; make sure the Preview box is checked so that you can see the changes in the Optimized image view as you drag the sliders. Click OK when you're satisfied.

7 You can compare the regular JPEG optimization with your weighted optimization in the 2-Up view. Here we've zoomed in to show a close up of the unweighted optimization (left) with the weighted optimization. Notice the artifacts around the text of the regular image, compared to the version with the weighted optimization.

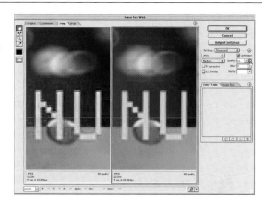

8 When you apply weighted optimization, Photoshop displays the upper end of the range of the custom setting in the appropriate text box, Quality in our example. Position the mouse cursor over the Channel button to see the actual range: "Channel Alpha 1 modifies quality between 30 and 65," in this example.

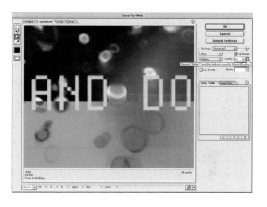

9 When you're satisfied, click the Optimize Menu button (the right-pointing arrow above the Lossy text box) and choose Save Settings. Give your custom optimization a name, click Save, and it will be available in the Settings pop-up menu for other images. Then click OK to save your image, and name your file in the Save Optimized As dialog box as prompted.

Enhancing Type with Layer Effects

Although most type on a Web page will be HTML, there are many times when you'll render it as a graphic—in navigational buttons, for example, or for corporate logos. On those occasions, you can have fun with your type using all of the tools at your disposal. We've already explored how you can get creative with type in Photoshop by applying vector transformations (see page 36); another option is to apply layer effects, such as drop shadows, glows, and bevels. The two features can work together or separately: The trick is that since you can't edit text after you convert it to a shape, you have to apply any desired styles before you apply vector transforms. Here we use layer effects to create a logo for a Web site of an imaginary client called Juiced; the technique can easily be applied to text for navigational buttons as well.

1 Create a new document in Photoshop, making it much larger than your actual text will be. Using the Type tool, click on the document and type the client's name. Specify the font (Cloister in our example), a Web-safe color, and other characteristics on the tool options bar. Photoshop automatically puts the type on its own Layer; click on it and Photoshop will rename it according to the text you've typed.

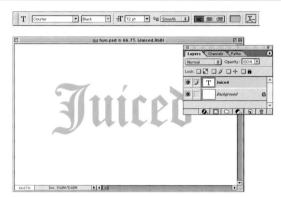

2 Double-click on the type layer to open the Layer Style dialog box. To apply an effect, select the name from the styles list and check the corresponding box. We applied a drop shadow, adjusting its angle but using all the other default options. Make sure the Preview box is checked so that you can see the effect in the image window.

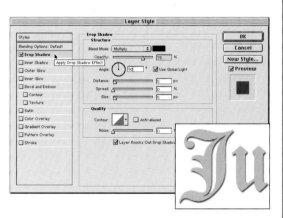

3 Experiment with other effects. We applied an Outer Glow, using a Web-safe orange, and then we applied a Bevel and Emboss. When you are satisfied with the results of your styled type, click OK. A list of the cumulative effects you used appears with the type layer on the Layers palette.

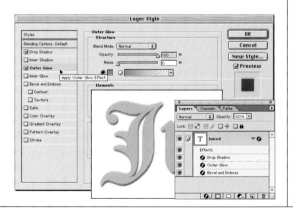

40

RELATED TIPS:

Managing Page Elements with Layer Styles, page 18
Formatting Type for Comps, page 32
Transforming Type Using Vectors, page 36

4 Now you can experiment with other fonts. Duplicate the type layer by choosing Duplicate Layer from the Layers palette pop-up menu. Then make a copy for each additional font you want to use. Select each duplicated layer individually and use the Move tool to position the contents in an empty area of your document.

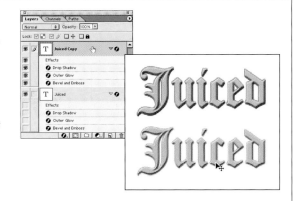

5 Double-click on the "T" on the Layers palette for your first duplicated layer. On the tool options bar, choose a different font (and different options, if you desire). If you're creating navigational buttons, change the text as well. (It's a good idea now to choose Layer Properties from the Layers palette pop-up menu and give the layer a logical name, such as the word and the typeface.)

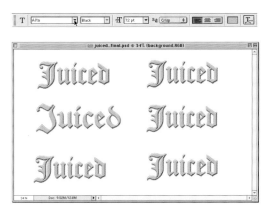

6 Repeat Step 5 for each duplicated type layer until you have experimented with all the fonts you want for your logo, or until you've created all of your navigational buttons.

7 Now you can add a special effects filter, such as a spotlight, behind your type. Select the background layer from the Layers palette and fill it with a color by choosing Fill from the Edit menu. Then choose Duplicate Layer from the Layers palette pop-up menu.

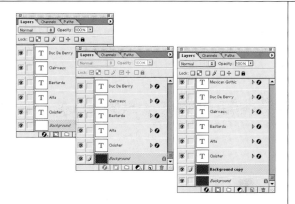

8 With the duplicated background layer selected, choose Render > Lens Flare from the Filter menu, choose a Brightness, Center, and Lens Type, and then click OK. You can drag the effect with the Move tool to see how it looks with different logos. Keep in mind that the Lens Flare will add non-Web-safe colors to the image, so save it as a JPEG and optimize the type using an alpha channel (see "Preserving Type in Bitmaps," page 38).

9 At any time, you can go back to any type layer, double-click on the "T," and edit the text or change the specs on the options bar. After we chose a final font, for example, we applied different warps to the text and changed the color of the first letter.

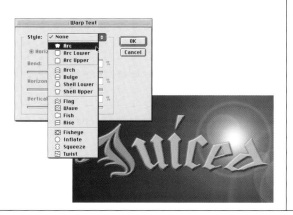

Specifying Fonts for Web Sites

Presenting text as a graphic has its place in Web design, but ultimately there's no way to avoid using HTML text on a Web page. The easiest way to format HTML text is with GoLive's font sets, which instruct a browser to use specific fonts to display a page. If the first typeface you specify isn't on the visitor's system, the browser looks for the second typeface, and so on. So if you want text to appear in Verdana but your visitor doesn't have it, you can specify the next best thing, such as Arial, as backup. That way, at least you can ensure that what you want to appear in a sans serif face doesn't become serif in the browser.

1 To specify font sets in GoLive, choose Font from the Type menu and then choose Edit Font Sets. In the Font Set Editor, select the Default icon in the left pane of the dialog box, and then click the New button under the Fonts Sets scrolling list to make a new set.

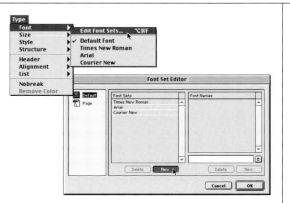

2 An empty font set called New Font Name appears in the Font Sets scrolling list. To add a font to the set, choose one from the pop-up menu under the Font Names list. The set name takes on the name of this font. To add another font, click the New button under the Font Names list and select another font from the menu. To specify a font that's not on your system, type the name into the text box. Click OK when you're finished.

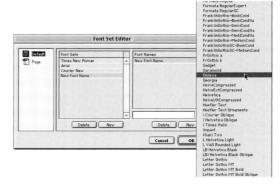

3 You have just added a global font set that will be available to all future documents you create. To see a list of your global font sets, choose Font from the Type menu. The sets are listed below the Edit Font Sets command.

RELATED TIPS:
Applying Style Sheets to HTML Pages, page 58
Understanding Style Sheet Attributes, page 112

Adobe GoLive 5.0

4 You can also create font sets for specific pages. Open a document and then open the Font Set Editor by choosing Font > Edit Font Sets from the Type menu. Click on the Page icon and then create your set. It will be available only to that document and will appear with the global sets under the Font command in the Type menu.

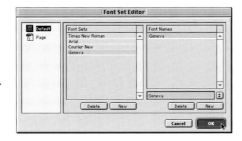

5 To create a font set for an entire site, choose New Site > Blank from the File menu to create the site, and then click the Font Sets tab in the site window that appears. From the Site menu, choose New and select Font Set, or drag a Font Set icon from the Site tab of the Palette onto the site window.

6 In the Font Set Inspector, name your set and press Return/Enter, and then select the fonts you want to include from the pop-up menu. When you're finished, you can view site-specific fonts sets in the Font Set Inspector, or look under the Font command in the Type menu.

7 To use your font sets, type some text into a document, select it, and choose the font set from the Font command under the Type menu. When you have multiple fonts specified in a set to use as a backup in case a browser can't display the first one, GoLive will display the first chosen font by default.

Understanding System Fonts

Although the problem isn't as bad as it used to be, consistent type on Web pages can be hampered by platform incompatibilities. The Mac OS and Windows 98/NT each install numerous fonts—the Mac OS installs 19 by default; Windows installs many more. Also, Microsoft Internet Explorer installs a number of fonts on the Mac, which brings the platform to close parity with what's available for Windows. But you can't ever be sure of what browser your visitors are using, or what fonts they have installed or activated in font utilities like ATM, so it's important to know the lowest common denominator when it comes to specifying HTML fonts. Below is a list of some system fonts for each platform; notice that only some fonts are common to both.

MAC OS 9.X		MICROSOFT WINDOWS 98/NT
Charcoal	New York	Arial
Chicago	Palatino	Courier New
Courier	Symbol	Symbol
Geneva	Times	Times New Roman
Helvetica	Verdana	Wingdings
Monaco		Verdana

Web Page Layout

Slicing Images for HTML Tables

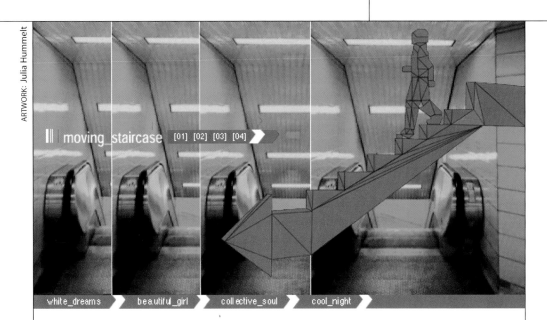

ARTWORK: Julia Hummelt

When you design Web pages composed of large images or backgrounds, there are two ways to make them display in a browser. One is to leave the image whole and provide navigational links and interactivity such as rollovers using an image map (see Making Image Maps, page 50). The second is to "slice" the large image into smaller pieces and fit each piece into an HTML table cell. The advantage to slices is that they load individually and quickly in the browser, keeping visitors engaged while they wait for the final composite to appear. Another advantage is that slices can be optimized individually—you can apply JPEG compression to an area of the page with a continuous-tone image, for example, and GIF compression to an area with text—potentially speeding the download process even more. And slices, which can be prepared in Photoshop or ImageReady, can contain hotspots with navigational links and rollovers, giving you all the flexibility and interactivity of image maps.

1 Photoshop and ImageReady let you create two types of slices: user-slices and layer-based slices. Functionally equivalent, they differ only in how they're created. When you create a slice with the Slice tool, it's called a user slice. To create one, choose the Slice tool and define the tool's style and other settings on the options bar. "Normal" lets you create slices by dragging the cursor in the image window.

2 When you create a slice from a layer in Photoshop or ImageReady, it's called a layer-based slice. To create one, select the layer you want to slice on the Layers palette and then choose New Layer Based Slice from the Layer menu. Photoshop and ImageReady create a slice around the visible pixels in that layer; transparent pixels are ignored.

3 Notice that any time you create a user-slice or layer-based slice, Photoshop and ImageReady automatically generate auto-slices for the remaining areas of the image. The slice you've created is bounded by a solid box, whose color you may specify on the options bar. Auto-slices are bounded by a dotted box. The programs also number the slices automatically, from top to bottom and left to right.

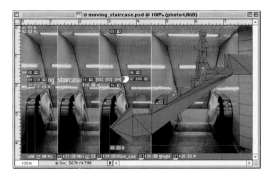

46

RELATED TIPS:

4 Auto-slices are regenerated anytime you edit or reposition a user-slice or layer-based slice. To prevent this from happening, or to optimize auto-slices individually, you must change them to user-slices. Choose the auto-slice with the Slice Select tool, and then click the Promote to User Slice button on the options bar in Photoshop; in ImageReady choose Promote to User-slice from the Slices menu.

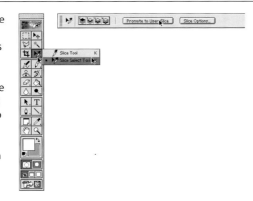

5 To set options for your user-slices or layer-based slices in Photoshop, select a slice with the Slice Select tool and click the Slice Options button on the options bar. In the Slice Options dialog box, you can name the slice, assign a URL link to make it a hotspot, or change its dimensions. In ImageReady, you define these options on the Slices palette. Note that if you specify options for an auto-slice, it is automatically promoted to a user-slice.

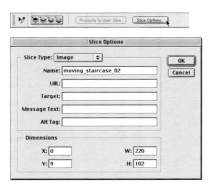

6 By default, slices are "image slices," meaning they contain image data. You can, however, set the slice Slice Type to No Image, which is appropriate for slices that contain a solid color or HTML text. These slices download more quickly, as you might imagine, but Photoshop and ImageReady don't preview their contents. For that, you have to use a browser.

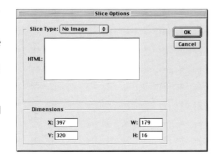

7 Finally, optimize your slices by choosing Save for Web from the File menu in Photoshop, or by accessing the Optimize palette as you experiment by choosing the 2-Up or 4-Up views from the optimized window views in either program.

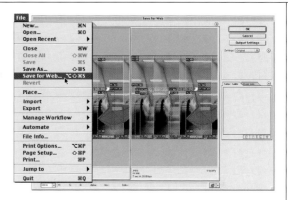

8 Now click on a slice to select it with the Slice Select tool, and then specify your optimization settings—a JPEG with Quality of 60, in this example. To apply the same settings to additional slices, Shift-click to select multiple slices.

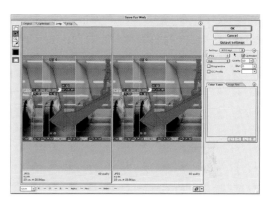

9 When you're satisfied, click OK. In the Save Optimized As dialog box, you can choose the format Images Only to save just the individual slices, but more likely you'll want to choose HTML and Images. That way the HTML code for the table, links, and so on, is saved with the slices and you don't have to recreate it. Name your file, and the program saves the slices in a folder called "Images."

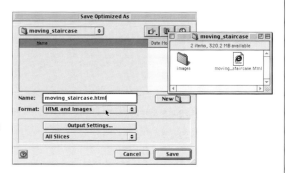

Optimizing Slices

ARTWORK: Zanne deJanvier

Slices display quickly but they can slow the display of the complete image because they make multiple server calls. That's why it's important to think strategically about not only how best to slice images for HTML tables, but also how best to optimize them. Depending on the content of your Web page, slices might not fall on a neat grid and will take some editing to suit your design; and depending on the content of each slice, you may want to optimize them differently to make the entire page download as efficiently as possible. In this example, we show you how to slice up a graphically complex Web page and how to appropriately optimize the slices using ImageReady. (You can also perform this slicing technique in Photoshop, using the Slice Options and Save for Web dialog boxes.)

1 Open the image file of your Web page comp in ImageReady. To define your slices, create a new layer over your flattened image by clicking on the Create New Layer button at the bottom of the Layers palette. Then draw the grid of your intended slices with the Line tool. On the options bar, click the Create Filled Region button and specify a relatively thin weight (ours is 2 pixels), with no anti-aliasing. Give the lines a color that contrasts well with your image.

2 To slice the image, use the Slice tool to drag along the lines you just drew. Create separate slices for areas that contain photos or gradations, areas of flat color, and vector-based artwork or text, or hyperlinks. To edit any slices created automatically, first select them with the Slice Select tool and then choose Promote to User-slice from the Slices menu. When you're finished, delete the layer containing the guide lines.

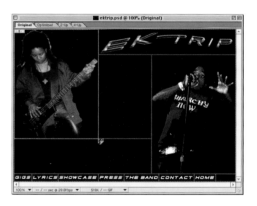

3 Select your slices with the Slice Select tool. Then on the Slice palette, indicate URL links and rename the slices if you don't like their default names. In this example, the image of the bass player will not be a link, but each of the words across the bottom of the image will be.

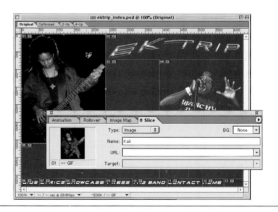

RELATED TIPS:
Slicing Images for HTML Tables, page 46
Understanding Color Palettes, page 104

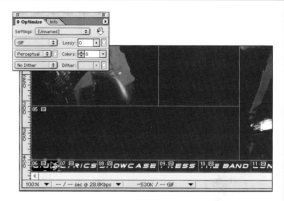

Adobe ImageReady 3.0   Adobe GoLive 5.0

4 To ensure the proper display of color in slices with flat color areas that match the HTML page background (black, in our example), select those slices with the Slice Select tool and choose No Image for the slice Type. Then set the background color (BG) to that of your HTML page (again, black in our example).

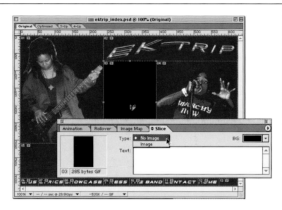

5 Once you've named and specified links for your slices, you can preview results as you optimize each slice by clicking on the Optimized tab of the image window.

6 Optimize the slices appropriately, starting with the photographic image in the left corner. Select it with the Slice Select tool and specify JPEG and appropriate quality settings on the Optimize palette. To optimize multiple slices at once—such as the slice of the bass player and the slice of the vocalist—Shift-click to select them both, and then apply your optimize settings.

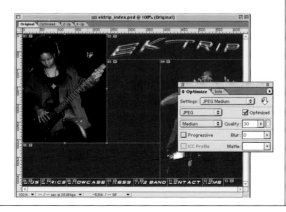

7 Optimize slices that contain text or graphic elements as GIFs. Here, we optimized the navigational links at the bottom of the image as 8-color GIFs using a perceptual palette and no dither.

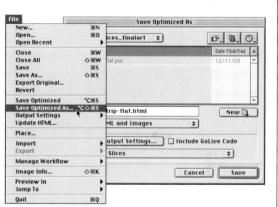

8 Choose Save Optimized As from the File menu and choose HTML and Images as your Format. ImageReady generates a folder containing the slices and an HTML file that positions them in a table.

9 Open the HTML file in GoLive, click on the Page icon in the Layout window, and set the page's background color to black in the Inspector. (If you don't know the exact shade of the background, use the Eyedropper or Magic Wand tool and the Info palette in ImageReady to view its hexadecimal values.) Click the Show in Browser button to preview your work.

Making Image Maps

Image maps let designers create Web pages that contain visually compelling messages and subtle functionality via "hotspot" links, which spare the designer from having to use boring and garish plain text links. The advantage of using image maps is that they can contain rectangular, round, or polygonal hotspots, compared to sliced images, which only support rectangular hotspots. Image map hotspots are typically based on layers in an image file and can be created in Illustrator, ImageReady, or GoLive. In our example, we created an imaginary landscape of several burning hotels; each building is actually a hotspot created in ImageReady that links to another Web page.

1 When you create your artwork, put each element that will have a hotspot on a separate layer. In this example, that means each hotel is on its own layer, apart from the background and from the text. Avoid overlapping hotspots, or hotspots with stray transparent pixels. If a browser encounters overlapping hotspots, it uses the one that appears first in the HTML code.

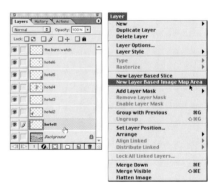

2 On the Layers palette, select the first layer containing an element that you want to be a hotspot and then choose New Layer Based Image Map Area from the Layer menu.

3 The Image Map palette automatically assigns a default name to your hotspot, but you can customize the name and define other specifications. For example, select a shape (a rectangle in our example) and specify the URL the hotspot will link to, and choose your target window if you're designing with frames. The URL appears in blue on the Layers palette, and your image window shows the boundaries of your hotspot.

RELATED TIPS:

4 Sometimes you'll need to define a polygonal hotspot, such as when the contents of the layer are a complex shape that closely adjoins an area that will be a hotspot from another layer. In that case, select Polygon from the Shape pop-up menu on the Image Map palette. ImageReady automatically creates a polygon closely hugs the object in the layer, but you can adjust the quality up or down to create a more or less complex shape.

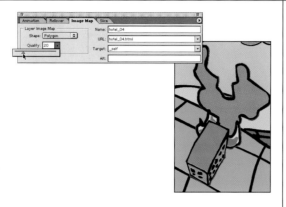

5 Although a polygonal hotspot creates a more dynamic shape, it's more difficult for visitors to hit, and it contains more HTML code. A rectangular shape, on the other hand, creates a hotspot that is easier to hit and also uses the least HTML code (only four coordinates are defined), which means browsers can display the page more quickly.

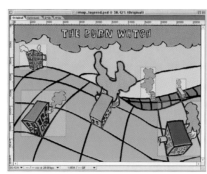

6 After you've defined your hotspots in every layer by repeating Steps 2, 3, and 4, it's time to optimize the image for the Web. On the Optimize palette, select the appropriate file format—GIF in our example. We started with a large palette—a 256-color Perceptual palette with no dithering because the image uses only flat color. Click the Optimized tab of the image window to see the results.

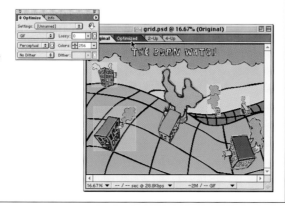

7 To keep Web-safe colors true while reducing the overall size of the image, we chose Select All Web Safe Colors from the Color Table palette's pop-up menu, and then clicked on the Lock button at the bottom of the palette. Then we reduced the number of colors in the image to 16.

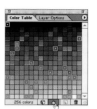

8 When you're satisfied, select Save Optimized As from the File menu, choose HTML and Images as your Format, and name your file with an .html suffix. ImageReady will generate the HTML code for the coordinates of the hotspots and the URL links, as well as save the actual image file. Drag the HTML file into a browser to see the image map you've created.

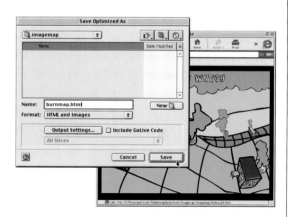

Creating Image Maps in GoLive

You can create image maps in GoLive 5.0, too. Begin by selecting an image on your Web page and then click on the More tab of the Image Inspector. Check the Use Map box and draw your hotspot by dragging on the page with one of the Region tools. Enter or browse for a URL link in the Inspector. Using the Actions palette, you can even attach triggered events to hotspots so that, for example, when someone positions a mouse over it a sound plays or a window opens. (For more on GoLive Actions, see "Creating Remote Rollovers," page 80.)

Designing Forms

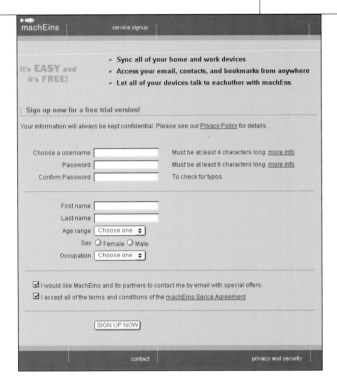

These days it's almost impossible to design a Web site that doesn't contain at least one form, whether it's to register visitors, conduct e-commerce, provide a search interface, or e-mail customer service. Nonetheless, forms make many Web designers nervous because browsers don't display them uniformly and because they require CGI scripts. Forms don't have to be daunting to design, however: Simply use an HTML table to ensure proper display and alignment, and use GoLive's Forms palette to drag and drop various elements—check and list boxes, for example—into table cells. You can then customize each element through the Inspector and have your Web server administrator help you write the CGI script.

1 Open your Web page or create one in GoLive. In Layout view, drag a Form icon from the Forms tab of the Objects palette onto your page.

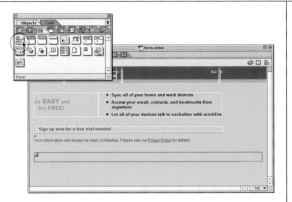

2 Then drag a Table icon from the Basic tab of the Objects palette into the form area of the page; for the name and password areas of this form, we'll start with the default 3-x-3 table.

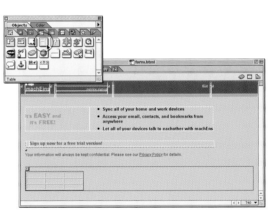

3 First create labels for the user name and password fields. Go back to the Forms tab of the Objects palette and drag a Label icon into each of the cells in the left column, and then type in the appropriate text. For our example, we chose "Choose a username," "Password," and "Confirm Password."

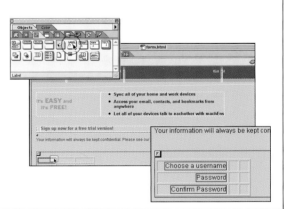

4 Drag a Text Field icon into each of the remaining table cells, and specify options for them on the Form Text Field Inspector. Use the Content field to add explanatory text for the visitor in the cells in the right column; use the Visible field to specify how many characters the visitor can see in each field.

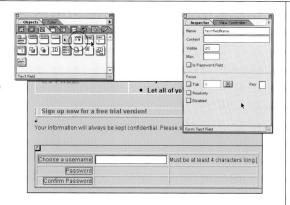

5 To add rows to the table, select it and specify more in the Table tab of the Inspector. Specify text positioning by selecting cells and using the Alignment pop-up menus in the Cell tab of the Inspector.

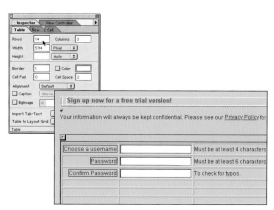

6 Add form elements by dragging and dropping icons from the Forms tab of the Objects palette into the appropriate cells of your table. We added labels, text fields, pop-up menus, radio buttons, check boxes, and a Submit button, which we relabeled "Sign Up Now." Specify options for each form element in the Inspector; for pop-up menus, for example, select a label from the list and type in the visitors' choice in the Label text box.

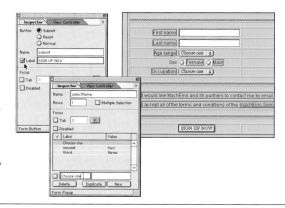

7 To let visitors advance to the next field in the form using the Tab key, choose Start Tabulator Indexing from the Special menu. This toggles on yellow boxes on each indexable element of your form. Click the elements successively; notice that the Inspector updates with each click, showing the index value in the Tab field as you go. Choose Stop Tabulator Indexing from the Special menu when you're finished.

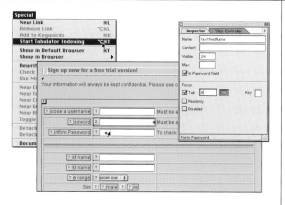

8 While we were designing, we kept the table border visible so that it was easy to select cells and rows. Now we'll set this border to zero so that it's invisible in the browser. However, you'll want to keep some padding around the cells so that the form elements have breathing room. We chose 2 pixels.

9 Check the form layout and elements, such as pop-up menus and lists, in the Preview window as well as in browsers, and fine-tune if necessary.

Creating Framed Web Pages

Frames provide a greater degree of flexibility and complexity to Web sites. They let browser windows display multiple HTML documents at once so that certain page elements stay visible onscreen while other content is updated and can be scrolled independently. They are ideal for global navigational buttons, as well as for banner ads and sidebars. They also ease navigation while speeding surfing for site visitors because certain elements are downloaded only once. To design a framed site, you must first create a frame definition document, which defines the layout of the site and is called the frameset. Then you create the associated frameset HTML pages. Using the Illustration section of a HOT designer's online portfolio as an example, we show you how.

1 Open a new document in GoLive and click on the Frame Editor tab of the document window.

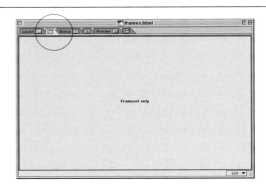

2 Click on the Frames tab of the Objects Palette to access a variety of template frameset layouts. Drag the icon with the layout you prefer into your document window; we chose a three-frame template to accommodate navigational buttons at the bottom and side of the page.

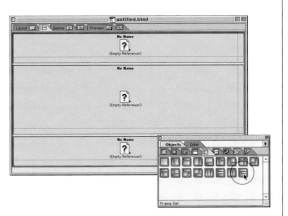

3 Customize templates by dragging additional frame icons onto the page and positioning as desired, as we did to create the middle-left frame here.

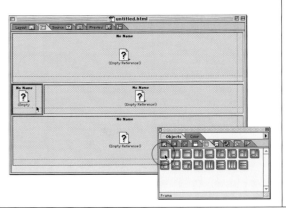

RELATED TIPS:
Slicing Images for HTML Tables, page 46
Making Framed Sites Searchable, page 56

4 Click inside the top frame to select it. Use the Browse button in the Frame Inspector to select the HTML document that will be associated with this frame. In this example, the file includes an embedded graphic. Since the graphic is static, fixed content, we set the frame height to that of the image inside, 62 pixels. Set Scrolling to No. Also, naming frames now will help when you define links later.

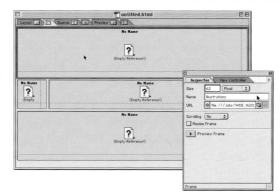

5 Click to select the middle-left frame and in the Frame Inspector use the Browse button to select your HTML file. Set scrolling to No and click the Preview button to see how your file appears. You'll need to resize this frame by dragging on the gray frame border. Click on the Preview button a second time to hide the file.

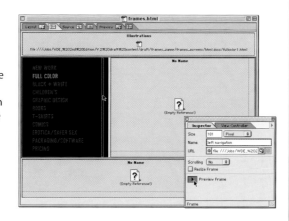

6 When one frame is sized absolutely (the middle-left frame in this case), another frame with the same orientation must be relative—or even the fixed frame will scale when a site visitor resizes the browser window. So click to select the middle-right frame and in the Frame Inspector, choose the HTML file that goes in it, and set the Size to Scale.

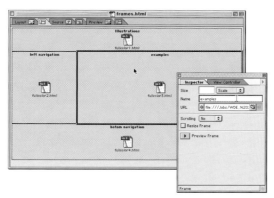

7 Select the remaining bottom frame and place the appropriate file in it, defining options on the Inspector as you go. You can preview your frames by clicking on the Frame Preview tab of the document window. You'll see that your frame borders are on.

8 To set frameset options, click a border in your main frame window. On the Frameset Inspector, set the BorderSize to 0 and the Border-Frame to No so that the borders don't appear in a browser. Leave BorderColor unchecked—since the borders don't show, you don't need to apply a color.

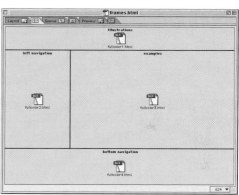

9 It's especially important to preview framesets in lots of browsers on multiple platforms. GoLive makes it easy to preview in all the browsers you may have on your system. Add them to the Browsers area of the Preferences dialog box, and then click and hold on the Show in Browser button for a pop-up list from which you can choose.

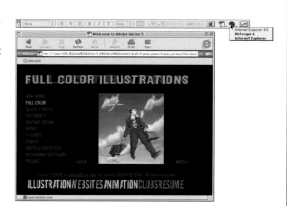

Making Framed Sites Searchable

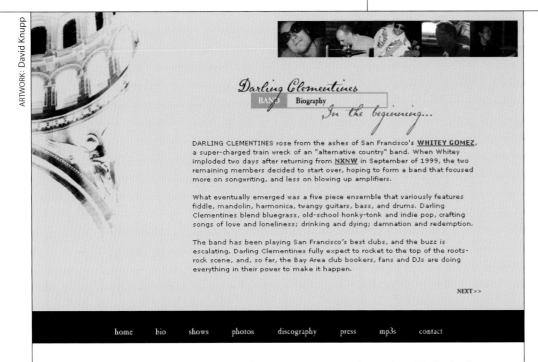

When you design a Web site using frames, you may unintentionally limit the searchability of your content. That's because search engine robots, which troll the Web in search of HTML documents to add to their indexes, frequently stop at the frameset definition document and never find their way to the content of the HTML documents inside the frames. Other times, search engines find just one framed content page, and if it doesn't have any navigational links, a visitor will have no way to access the rest of your site. Short of avoiding frames altogether, there are two ways to solve this problem. The first involves adding searchable keywords to the frameset page through metatags, keywords and comment tags; the second involves forcing browsers to always display framed content pages within their frameset, thus preserving the site's structure.

1 Open the frameset document in GoLive. In the Layout view, click the triangle to left of the Page icon to open its head section. Then open the Head tab of the Objects Palette.

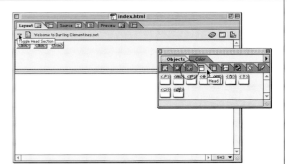

2 Drag the keywords placeholder icon into the frameset page's head section.

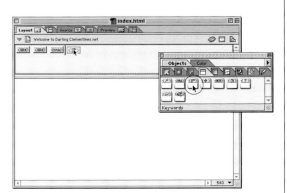

3 Click on the icon to open the Keywords Inspector. Add as many keywords and phrases as you wish, including the typical search terms you think your prospective visitors might use.

RELATED TIPS:
Creating Framed Web Pages, page 54

4 Some search engines index comment tags, so drag the Comment icon from the Head tab of the Objects palette to the frameset's head section, as you did with the Keywords icon. Then double-click on the Comment icon to open the Comments Inspector, and type in your text.

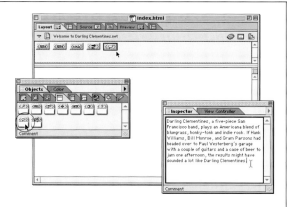

5 Now open one of the HTML content pages referenced in the frameset page of your site, and again click the triangle next to the Page icon in the Layout view to open the head section of the document.

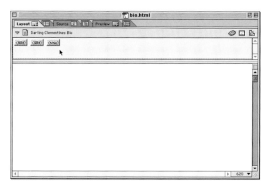

6 From the Smart tab of the Objects palette, drag a Head Action icon into the head section of the document, and then click on it to open the Action Inspector.

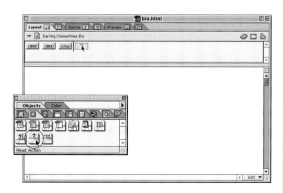

7 On the Inspector, choose OnLoad from the Exec. pop-up menu and choose ActionPlus > ForceFrame from the Actions pop-up menu. Click on the Browse button to select the frameset document for the Frameset field. This tells a browser that when it loads this HTML page, even from a search engine link, it should always be displayed within its frameset.

8 Repeat Steps 5 through 7 for all of your HTML content pages, and then save them and the frameset page.

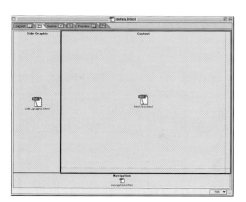

Customizing Search Engine Descriptions

Search engines often return short descriptions of sites they locate along with the URL. By default, most display the first 20 to 40 words of your page, including <ALT> tags. This may not always be useful or appropriate for your visitors, so use a metatag instead: Drag a Metatag icon from the Head tab of the Objects palette into the head section of your HTML document. In the Meta Inspector, change the word in the Name field from "generic" to "description," and then write the appropriate description in the Content box.

ARTWORK: David Knupp

1 With a new HTML document open in GoLive, click the Page icon in the document window and set the basic properties in the Page Inspector. Place images and type text on the page, not worrying about exact positioning for the time being. Avoid using tables and frames when you know you'll be applying a style sheet; they complicate positioning.

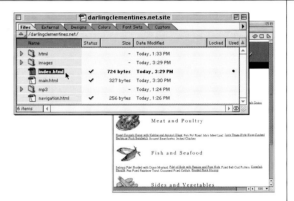

2 Create URL links by selecting text or graphics, clicking the New Link button on the toolbar, and specifying the URL on the Link tab of the Text or Image Inspector. Save the document.

3 Choose New Special from the File menu and open a new Style Sheet Document. You will use this style sheet document to apply formatting to the page you just prepared.

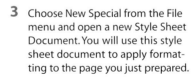

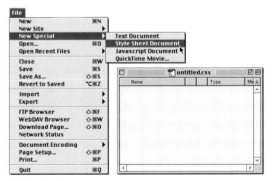

Cascading style sheets, like style sheets used in page layout programs for print, let designers control the appearance and positioning of type and graphics on the Web. You can, for example, create headline, paragraph, and banner styles that specify how text and graphics should be displayed relative to the browser window or to other page elements. You can specify attributes such as the size, spacing, and color of text as well as the spacing and margins for images and graphics. (For a guide to cascading style sheets (CSS) capability in GoLive, see "Understanding Style Sheet Attributes," page 112.) Style sheets make it easy to keep designs consistent across pages, but apply them cautiously: Different browsers support different CSS attributes, so test pages extensively to be sure that what you design is what visitors see.

RELATED TIPS:

Specifying Fonts for Web Sites, page 42
Understanding Style Sheet Attributes, page 112

4 Click the New Class Selector button on the toolbar (the far-left button, with a dot in the middle) to create a new style class. In the CSS Selector Inspector, name the class in the Basics tab; the name should describe the properties of the class or what it is modifying. We called ours ".mastheadgraphic" because it will be used to position the masthead graphic. (Note: Class styles names must begin with a period.)

5 Click the Position tab in the CSS Selector Inspector. To ensure that the masthead graphic appears in the upper-left corner of the browser window, we set the Positioning Kind to Absolute, specifying the Left and Top values as 0 pixels. Because style classes with absolute positioning are separate from the main document, the masthead will reside on a "layer" above the other page elements.

6 Create a second style class to position the table of contents graphic. Name it ".toc_graphic" in the Basics tab of the CSS Selector Inspector, and switch to the Block tab. Set the top margin to 110 pixels so that it falls 10 pixels below the masthead graphic, which is 100 pixels tall. Set the left margin to allow for some extra space. We chose 162 pixels, which will align the graphic with the section header titles below.

Table of Contents

7 Now it's time to position the section header graphics. Create a new style class and name it ".sectionheadergraphic," with a top margin of 10 pixels and a left margin of 30 pixels. This will position each section header graphic 10 pixels below the previous block and will maintain the 30-pixel offset from the left side of the browser window.

Desserts and Pastries

8 Create a fourth style class for the recipe titles, naming it ".recipes." Set a top margin of –15 pixels, which moves the text up 15 pixels, closing up some space between the text and the bottom of the section header graphic above. (Use caution here. You can move the text up too far, so the graphic above obscures it and any links that are hidden will not be accessible.) Use the left margin of 162 pixels to position it below the section titles; we chose a right margin of 10%.

9 Since this style class will format text, switch to the Font tab of the CSS Selector Inspector. Select Maroon in the Color field, and set the Size to 0.75 em. Specify a font family by clicking on the New button and choosing a primary font from the pop-up menu. Specify alternate faces also, and end the list with a generic family name, such as san serif.

Wintermelon Soup, Perfect
& Leek Consomme, Frilly French
rley, New England Style Quahog
g Noodle

Applying Style Sheets to HTML Pages

10 To specify a color for URL text links, set a link tag style. Click the New Element Selector button on the toolbar (the one with the greater than and less than symbols). Name the style "a," the HTML tag used to designate anchors, in the Basics tab of the CSS Selector Inspector. Specify the properties on the Font tab: Select Red for the color, set the weight to Bolder, and check None under Decoration, which removes the underline that usually denotes a hyperlink in a browser.

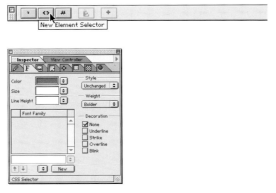

11 Select the anchor style tag you just created, click the Duplicate button in the toolbar, and name the new style "a:hover." This style, which will be applied to a text link, changes the color of the text when the mouse cursor is positioned over it. (In our example, we set the color to Purple.)

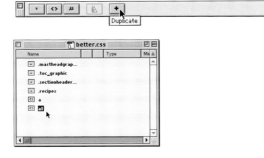

12 Save the style sheet with a .css extension and in an appropriate folder in your site's local directory.

13 To apply the style sheet to your HTML document, you must link them. Click the Open CSS Interface button at the top right of your HTML document window (the button with the stair-step icon) to access the empty style sheet window for your document. Control/right-click and choose Add Link to External CSS from the context-sensitive menu that appears.

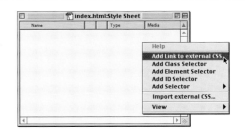

14 Click on the empty reference document that appears in the External folder and then browse to select your style sheet in the External Style Sheet Inspector.

15 The link tag style will be applied to links automatically, but you have to manually apply the style classes. Start from the bottom of your HTML document and work upward. Select the last set of recipes. In the Style tab of the Text Inspector, check the style ".recipes" as a Div, which is short for division and refers to a selected section of text. Apply this style to the other recipes as well.

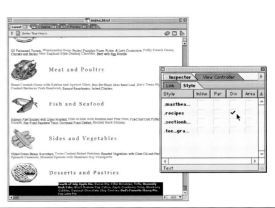

60

RELATED TIPS:

Specifying Fonts for Web Sites, page 42
Understanding Style Sheet Attributes, page 112

16 Now select the last section header graphic by dragging the I-beam cursor from left to right across it, which lets position the graphic as an inline element. Apply the style ".sectionheadergraphic" as a division in the Style tab of the Text Inspector. Repeat for the other section headers.

17 Select the table of contents graphic and apply its style in the Text Inspector. A large space will appear above the date that allows for the masthead graphic and the 10-pixel offset that you specified in the style.

18 Finally, apply the style for the masthead. To see the graphic's absolute positioning, switch to the Preview tab of the document window, or choose Show in Browser from the Special menu.

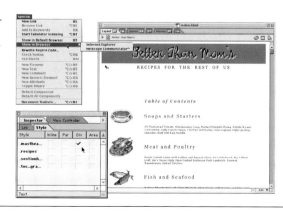

19 Preview the page in as many browsers as possible, since different browsers on the Mac and in Windows display style sheets differently (or sometimes not at all, in older software). If you don't have access to multiple versions of browsers on multiple platforms, click on the Page icon in Layout view to access the Page Inspector, and choose the View Controller tab. Tab over to the Preview document window, and then choose from among the options in the Root CSS pop-up menu. GoLive approximates the preview of your HTML page for various browsers.

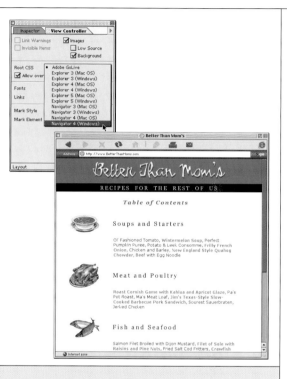

Naming CSS Elements

When creating and applying CSS styles, choose a naming convention carefully. Web browsers are often unable to decipher style names that include spaces or nonalphanumeric characters such as underscores and hyphens. Style names are case insensitive and should always begin with a letter.

One exception is the use of colons, which can be used to delineate several behaviors of a single class. For instance, the anchor tag has four pseudoclasses. The default behavior of a hypertext link is determined by naming the style "a:link"; "a:visited" defines the properties of a visited link; "a:active" and "a:hover" are considered dynamic pseudoclasses that change the characteristics of links as they are clicked or as the mouse cursor hovers over them.

Designing Pages Using Smart Objects

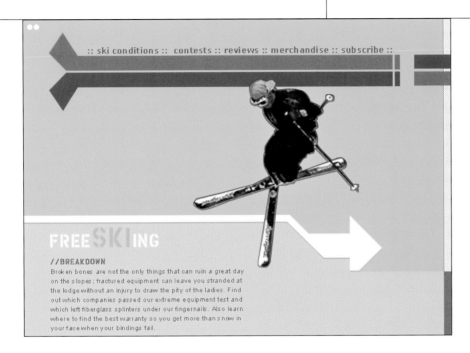

 Managing the images and graphics you create using myriad applications is one of those Web tasks that leaves even the most experienced designers pulling their hair out. Just think about all the slices, animations, and image maps you generate using Photoshop, Illustrator, and LiveMotion. Thankfully, GoLive 5.0 has a feature, Smart Objects, that makes designing pages with these files much easier. When you import a file created in another Adobe application into GoLive using Smart Objects, GoLive creates a Web-safe copy that is linked to the source file. Need to tweak an image now that you see it in context? Simply double-click on the Smart Object to open the source file in the application where it was created, make and save your edit, and the (smart) Web-safe version in GoLive automatically reflects the changes. Here, we show you how Smart Objects work using a Web page that was comped in Photoshop and optimized in ImageReady.

1 With a blank document open in GoLive, click the Smart tab on the Objects palette and drag a Smart Photoshop, Smart Illustrator, or Smart LiveMotion icon onto your page. We chose Smart Photoshop because that's where our comp was designed.

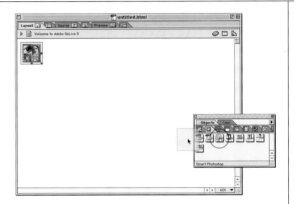

2 Choose Window > Inspector to view the Live Image Inspector if it isn't already open, and in the Basic tab, browse to select your Source file. Smart Photoshop objects should be RGB PSD files so that you can go back and edit the original layered file if necessary. GoLive does not recognize any attached interactivity, such as rollover effects or animations, but sliced images are OK. (Use the Save, not Save for Web, command in Photoshop.) Click Open.

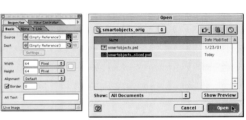

3 Because we are placing a sliced PSD image, GoLive prompts us to save the "smart" (duplicate) image, to which it appends a .data file extension. Save this target information in your site folder.

RELATED TIPS:

Importing Artwork for Animation, page 72

4 When you place Smart Photoshop objects, GoLive automatically displays the Save for Web dialog box, where you can optimize your image or slices if you haven't already done so. Click OK when you're done. (If your Smart Object isn't sliced, you'll be prompted to save the target file now.)

5 Some solid-color slices in our image contain no data, just a background color (which we specified in the Slice palette in ImageReady). That's OK. The document does not display correctly in GoLive's Layout view, but it will look fine in a browser. Notice that an icon for the associated application appears in the bottom-right corner of the Smart Object—ours shows ImageReady because we optimized our slices there after designing the page in Photoshop.

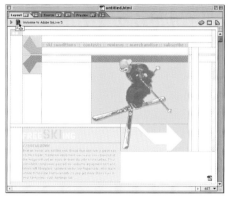

6 Click on the Page icon to edit your document settings. In the Inspector, give your page a title (so that it doesn't display "Adobe GoLive" in the browser's title bar—a rookie mistake) and set the Margin Width and Height to zero so that your image will be flush with the top left corner of the browser window. Then choose a background color that matches the original background of your image.

 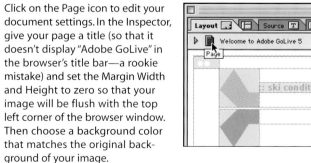

7 Inevitably, one of your site editors will inform you that the text in the image needs to be replaced. Since you've used Smart Objects, it's easy to make this fix: Double-click on the Smart Object icon to edit the source file in the associated application, or Control-click/right-click for a context-sensitive menu that lets you choose either Photoshop or ImageReady.

8 In ImageReady, use the Type tool to make the requested changes, then choose Save from the File menu when you're finished. (You must overwrite the previous version, rather than using Save As, to maintain GoLive's Smart Link to the file.)

9 Return to GoLive, which will have automatically updated the Smart Object on your page. Preview the document in a browser to see not only your changes but also the correct background colors.

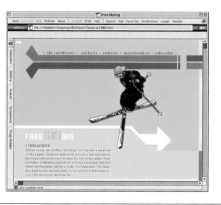 

Active Elements

Chapter 4

Animating GIFs

You don't need to learn JavaScript or use a sophisticated 3D or video application to stimulate visitors' interest in your Web site. Animated GIFs can make text or simple graphics dance across your Web pages. These files, which are simply sequences of slightly varying frames that display successively to make an animation, are small and don't require a browser plug-in to be viewed. In ImageReady, animated GIFs are based on layers, so the first task is to create a multilayered image in Illustrator or Photoshop and then edit the individual layers—changing an object's opacity, position, and other attributes—to create frames of motion in ImageReady. Here we show you how by making a ring of colored parallelograms spin around in a circle.

1 With your file open on the Original window tab, choose Show Animation from the Window menu to access the Animation palette. The thumbnail shows the contents of the first frame of the animation: The frame contains all visible layers in your image, so toggle on just those that you want to be in the starting frame by clicking the appropriate eye icons in the Layers palette. Here, we initially hide the circle of blue diamonds, but we'll return to it later.

2 To create a second frame, click the Duplicate Current Frame button at the bottom of the Animation palette. As you add and edit frames, remember that each frame contains all visible layers, and that the document window always displays the contents of the frame chosen in the Animation palette.

3 Now we're ready to animate the circle of green diamonds; we will make it spin 360 degrees. In the second frame, we select the layer that contains the component we want to animate ("green circle"), choose Duplicate Layer from the Layers palette pop-up menu, and make our desired adjustments—rotate it 30 degrees by choosing Edit > Transform > Rotate.

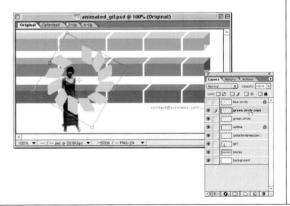

RELATED TIPS:
Creating Complex Animations, page 68
Animating Rollovers, page 78

Adobe ImageReady 3.0

4 Keep the duplicated layer visible but toggle off visibility of the unedited layer. The second frame is done.

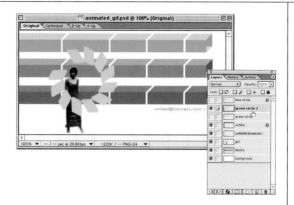

5 Now we repeat Steps 2 through 4 until the circle makes a full 360-degree rotation. This results in 13 total frames and layers—the original position plus 12 intermediate positions. In each frame, we make sure that the duplicate layer (which contains the repositioned circle) is visible and that all other intermediate positions are hidden.

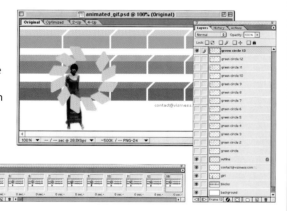

6 You can make changes to multiple frames at once by Shift-clicking to select them. With odd-numbered frames selected (Command/Ctrl-click them), we set the delay to 0.1 seconds by clicking on the Delay value below the selected frame in the Animation palette to access the pop-up menu.

7 Specify whether you want your animation to loop once, a specific number of times, or continuously by choosing an option from the pop-up menu at the bottom of the Animation palette.

8 Preview your animation at anytime by clicking on the Play button at the bottom of the Animation palette, or preview it in a browser by choosing File > Preview In and choosing a desired browser.

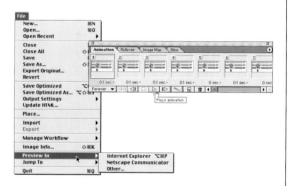

9 When you're satisfied, optimize the animation as you would any non-animated GIF using the Optimize palette.

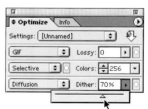

Creating Complex Animations

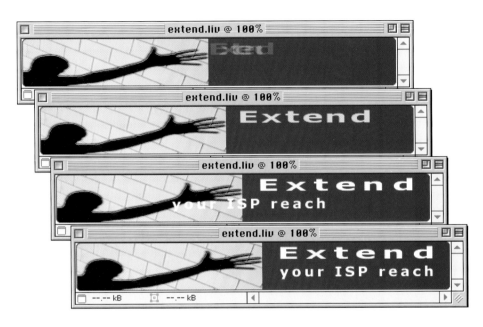

Creating animated GIFs in ImageReady is a great way to add some basic interactivity to your Web pages, but if you want to get sophisticated—animating multiple objects, for example, or animating discrete attributes of objects—you'll want to use LiveMotion. LiveMotion works with the concept of compositions, which contain objects and shapes that are animated individually or as a group along a timeline. You can instruct objects to fade in and out, move across the page, trigger events, and much more. You can even import artwork that you've created in Photoshop or Illustrator and either use it as a background in a composition or convert the layers into objects and animate them (see "Importing Artwork for Animation," page 72). Here we'll show you how to import some artwork for a banner ad background, and then add and animate a couple of lines of text, making the text fade in and out and move across the page.

1 Create the bitmapped background for the ad in Photoshop: Ours is a 470-x-61-pixel RGB image, half of which contains a solid blue fill and half of which contains a stock photo image.

2 Since we're not animating the layers in this artwork, flatten the layers and save as a PSD file.

3 Launch LiveMotion and choose File > New to create a new composition. Make the composition's dimensions the same as your Photoshop background. The default 12-frames-per-second speed suffices for most animations; choose Auto-Layout from the Export pop-up menu and check the Make HTML box so that when you export your composition, LiveMotion slices it and saves it in an HTML table.

RELATED TIPS:
Animating GIFs, page 66
Creating Animation Styles, page 74

4 Choose File > Place and browse to select your Photoshop image. Then choose Timeline > Show Timeline Window. Here you'll see each object in the composition listed, including the background you just imported.

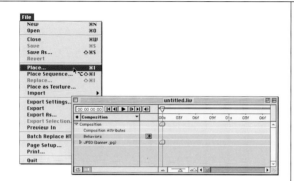

5 Begin adding and animating the ad's text. Select the Type tool and choose a color for the text from the Colors palette (we chose white), and then click on the composition with the Type tool.

6 In the Type Tool dialog box that appears, choose a font and specify attributes such as size and alignment, and then type your text in the box—the word *Extend*, in our example. Click OK. Note that the sample text in the dialog box appears black even if you chose another color, such as white, for your text.

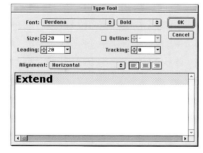

7 Drag with the Selection tool and/or use the arrow keys to position the text in the composition. Drag the bounding box to stretch the text; double-click the text to access the Type Tool dialog box and edit it; or use the Properties palette to change the text's properties.

8 Look at the timeline again. Notice that your text appears as an object, named by its color and its contents; click the arrow to the left of the object name to view its attributes —position, rotation, opacity, and so on. Each of these aspects of the object can be animated. Since we plan to animate the letters individually, click the "Extend" object and choose Object > Break Apart Text. Now we have six objects in the timeline—one for each of the letters in the word *Extend*.

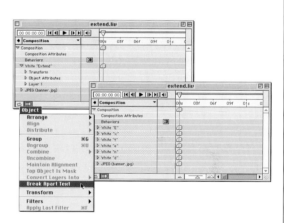

9 Set the duration of the entire animation by selecting Composition and dragging the duration bar slider to 2 seconds.

Creating Complex Animations

10 To make the letters in *Extend* move in from a single origin at the left side of the solid blue background, Shift-click in the timeline to select all of the letters, then drag to position the current time marker at the end point of their animation, 1 second 6 frames in our example. Create a keyframe by choosing Timeline > New Keyframe > New Position Keyframe.

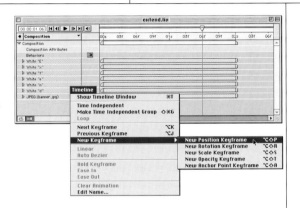

11 Drag the current time marker back to 0 seconds and, with the letters still selected, enter their starting x-position (225) in the Transform palette. This generates a starting keyframe; LiveMotion will automatically create the intermediate frames of motion between these keyframes. With the current time marker at 0, the letters appear positioned on top of one another at their origin point in the composition window.

12 Preview the animation you've just created by clicking the Play button in the timeline.

13 Add the next block of text—the tag line, *your ISP reach*—by using the Type tool as described in Steps 5 through 7. We're going to make this text fly in from the far-left side of the ad after *Extend* is fully displayed.

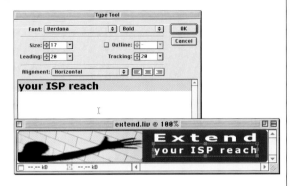

14 While the text is sitting where it was created (which is where we want it to end up), drag the current time marker to 2 seconds and create the final position keyframe by choosing Timeline > New Keyframe > New Position Keyframe. Then drag the current time marker and the left (start) duration slider to 1 second 6, and then drag the object off the left side of the composition. This automatically creates a starting position keyframe.

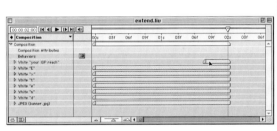

15 Preview the entire animation so far by clicking the Play button in the timeline, or by clicking the Preview Mode button (with the pointing-finger icon) in the toolbar.

RELATED TIPS:

16 To finesse the animation, we'll make the letters in *Extend* fade in as they move across the background. Select the first letter, *E*, position the current time marker at 0 seconds, and click the stopwatch icon next to the Opacity attribute to set a starting keyframe for the fade. In the Opacity palette, set the Object Opacity to 0.

17 Move the current time marker to the point where the letter reaches its final position (1 second 6) and set the Object Opacity to 100 in the Opacity palette. This automatically creates an ending keyframe for the fade.

18 Repeat Steps 15 and 16 for the letters *x, t, e, n,* and *d*. In our example the letters reach their final fade at intervals of 2 to 3 frames.

19 By default, the animation will play once and end; if you want it to play continuously, select Composition in the timeline and click the loop button in the lower-left-hand corner.

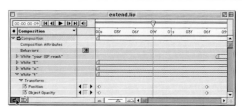

20 When satisfied, choose File > Save, and then choose File > Export. Since we specified in Step 1 that we want to save the composition with HTML, LiveMotion supplies an HTML extension automatically. To view or change export file formats, choose File > Export Settings and edit the settings on the Export palette.

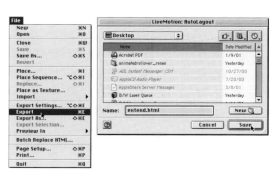

Importing Artwork for Animation

Although LiveMotion offers an assortment of drawing tools with which you can create original animated compositions, you can also create your comps in Photoshop or Illustrator and then import them into LiveMotion to create dynamic animations that involve movement, transformations, and transparency. This way, you can work as you have always done—creating multilayered files with bitmapped images, text, and graphics, and when you import the files into LiveMotion, you simply convert the layers into objects and create your animation. Here's how to prepare an Adobe Illustrator comp for animation in LiveMotion.

1 Create your vector-based artwork in Illustrator. For example, we drew this scene of a house on a hill, in which each element of the image resides on an individual layer.

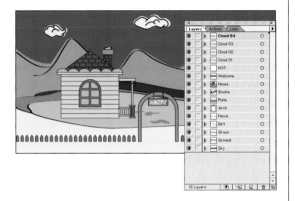

2 Save your file by choosing Save from the File menu. In the Save dialog box name the file and choose Adobe Illustrator document from the Format pop-up menu.

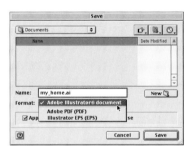

3 The Illustrator Native Format Options dialog box appears. Because of an incompatibility between Illustrator 9.0 and LiveMotion 1.0, choose Illustrator 8.0 from the Compatibility pop-up menu, and then click OK. If an alert window displays a warning, ignore it and click OK.

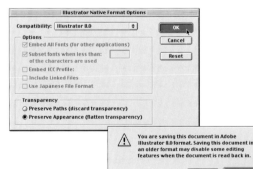

72

RELATED TIPS:

Creating Complex Animations, page 68
Creating Animation Styles, page 74

Adobe LiveMotion 1.0   Adobe Illustrator 9.0

4 Launch LiveMotion and choose File > New. In the Composition Settings dialog box, make the composition the size of your Illustrator image, 700 x 360 pixels in our example.

5 Now import your Illustrator artwork by choosing File > Place. Browse to select the file from the LiveMotion: Place dialog box, then click Open.

6 Choose Timeline > Show Timeline Window. In the Timeline window, you'll see the composition and its attributes and behaviors, as well as an EPS object—your placed Adobe Illustrator file.

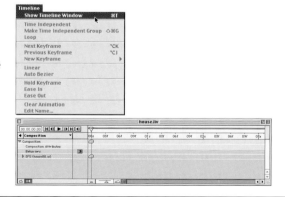

7 LiveMotion imports Illustrator (and Photoshop) files as single, one-layered objects, but it remembers all of the layers that were saved in the original application. To access and work with those layers as individual objects, choose Object > Convert Layers Into > Objects.

8 In the Timeline, notice that the EPS object has been replaced by one object for each converted layer. Although LiveMotion doesn't maintain the original layer names for these objects, the order of objects in LiveMotion is the same as the order of the layers in Illustrator.

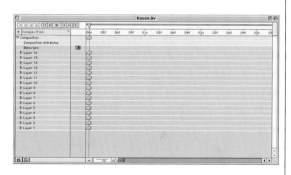

9 Take a few moments to give the objects intuitive names. You can click on one to select it; a bounding box will appear around the object in the composition window to identify it. Choose Timeline > Edit name and enter the new name for the object. You may want to refer to the original Illustrator file to help you. Now you're ready to animate.

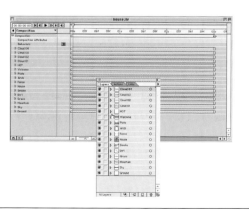

Creating Animation Styles

Once you get the hang of creating animations in LiveMotion you'll no doubt want to start using the software's styles feature. Like styles in Illustrator or Photoshop, styles in LiveMotion describe a set of attributes, such as effects, colors, and animations. In LiveMotion styles are associated with a particular object, and they can contain up to 99 object layers, each of which can have a combination of color, background fill, texture, 3D effect, and any attributes set in the Filter or Layer palette. Styles do not describe what the object is (geometric, text, or image), its shape, transformations, Web palette settings, or behaviors. But they make it easy to quickly apply a group of attributes to multiple objects, saving time and ensuring consistency from one object to another.

1 Create a composition with an object whose attributes you want to save as a style. Here we're making a banner ad from a background imported from Photoshop; it features several lines of animated text. We type the first word, *Differentiate*, and apply a 6-frame fade. We'll save its layer and animation attributes as a style.

2 Select the text and open the Styles palette. Choose a view from the pop-up menu: Swatches, Preview, or Name; the last displays a list of style names with a small thumbnail of each. Then click the buttons at the bottom of the palette to choose which styles you want to view: We narrow down the list to Object Layer and Animation styles, because the one we create will contain both animation and layer attributes.

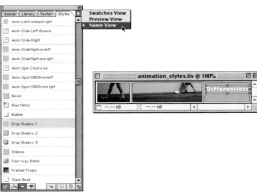

3 Click the New Style button at the bottom of the palette. In the dialog box that appears, name your style ("Differentiate_Fade" in our example), and check the Layers and Object Animation/Rollover boxes. Uncheck "Ignore color of first layer." Click OK. The new style contains the layer attributes (the color, effects, fills, and so on,) as well as the animation attributes (the 6-frame fade-in) of the word *Differentiate*.

74

RELATED TIPS:

Managing Page Elements with Layer Styles, page18
Drawing a Navigation System, page 26

Adobe LiveMotion 1.0

4 To apply this style to other text, first position the current time marker where you want it to begin to fade in, and then type the text into the composition with the Type tool (we wrote the word *yourself*). Then choose the style from the palette and click the Apply Style button.

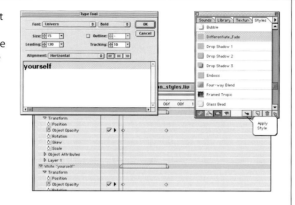

5 Then we apply the style to the rest of text objects: *from the/dot/snobs./ AgencyUgly.com/Click here/to/ ENTER*. Note that applying a style removes all previous attributes.

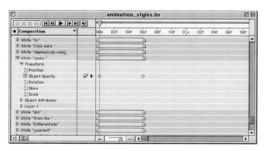

6 After you've applied the style to the entire message, you may find that the sequence is not correctly timed. Objects may be timed to appear after the composition ends, certain words may fade in on top of others, or fades may not begin and end exactly when you want them to.

7 First we make the entire composition 3 seconds long. Then we want the words *Differentiate yourself* to disappear after the visitor has read them and be replaced by *from the dot snobs*. So we position the right (end) duration bar slider for *Differentiate* and *yourself* at frame 11, at which point they disappear from the composition; we also change the timing of the fade of the word *yourself* by dragging the start keyframe to frame 5 and the end keyframe to frame 8.

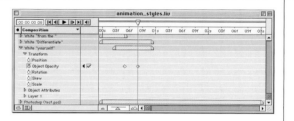

8 Continue to adjust the keyframes and duration bar sliders for each object until you are satisfied. In our example, we removed the fade-ins from many of the objects (by deleting the keyframes) so that the end of the message—*dotsnobs/ AgencyUgly.com/Click here to ENTER*—flash onscreen.

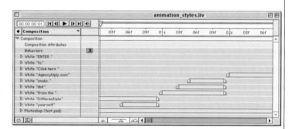

9 When you're done, choose File > Export Settings and make sure SWF is your file format. Then choose File > Export to save your composition.

Animating with DHTML

Another technique for adding animation to your Web page is to use DHTML. DHTML animations, which are supported by Netscape Navigator and Internet Explorer 4.x and later, can be produced in GoLive without programming. The software's "floating boxes" hold objects that can move along a path that you designate, as well as fade in and out, either by dragging the box across the page or by specifying exact coordinates at specific keyframes and letting the software create the in-between frames. Objects can be images, text, or even Java applets. You can execute the following technique, in which we animate a fish swimming across a page, with any object you've created and saved in a Web-friendly format.

1 Launch GoLive and drag an Image icon from the Objects palette into the blank, untitled document. In the Basic tab of the Image Inspector, browse to select the Source image that you want to appear as your page background. Ours is a GIF prepared in Photoshop.

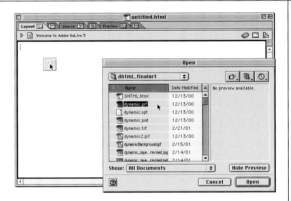

2 Drag a Floating Box icon from the Objects palette onto your page and position it where you want the animation to begin.

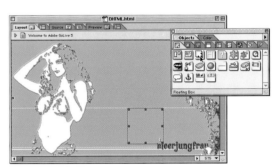

3 Next, choose the image you want to appear in the floating box; in our example, it's an illustration of a fish. Select the floating box in your layout, and check the BGImage box in the Inspector. Then browse to select the image.

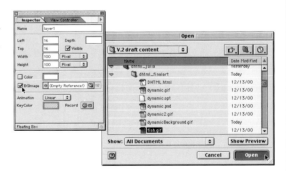

76

RELATED TIPS:
Importing Artwork for Animation, page 72

4 Give the floating box an intuitive name so that you will know what you are animating.

5 Click on the Open DHTML Time-line Editor button (with the film-strip icon) at the top right of your document window. The timeline initially displays one track and a single, starting keyframe for the animation.

6 Click to select the keyframe (the rectangle marker with the circle inside) in the timeline and then click to select the floating box in the document window. Drag the floating box to its starting point; in our example, we actually dragged it off the document so that the fish will enter from the right side of the page.

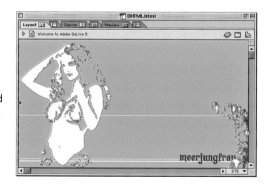

7 Drag the time cursor to 15 and then Command/Ctrl-click in the timeline to add a keyframe. Drag the floating box in the document window to the position where it should be 15 seconds into the animation.

8 Add more keyframes and positions so that the fish "swims" across the page. To make the fish swim smoothly, Shift-click to select all the keyframes and choose Curve from the Animation pop-up window in the Inspector. Use the buttons in the Timeline editor to control play-back: Enhance it by increasing the default speed of 15 frames per second, and specify whether the animation should loop forever or bounce back and forth.

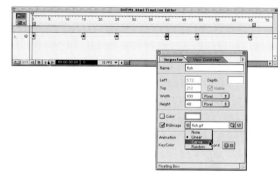

9 Preview the animation at any time by clicking the Play button.

Animating Rollovers

Rollovers are effects such as glows, color changes, or sounds that occur when the mouse cursor is rolled over an object. They are a compelling way to add interactivity to a Web page: You can, for example, reposition elements of a graphic or add text to enhance the graphic. Rollovers can be created in several Adobe applications, including ImageReady and LiveMotion, and they involve working with object states—the "normal," or off, state is what the site visitor sees before the mouse triggers the effect; the "on," or over, state, is what the visitor sees when the effect is triggered. As with the frames of animated GIFs created in ImageReady, the states of rollover effects are based on layers. You first have to create the layered image in Illustrator or Photoshop and then you define the rollover effects in ImageReady. Here we show you how.

1 When you create your art in Photoshop, put the default (off) states and the rollover (on) states of each object on a separate layer. In this example, the off states are the large pieces of fruit; the on states will be small pieces. Then toggle on visibility for only those layers that will be part of your animation.

2 Click the Jump to ImageReady button at the bottom of the Photoshop toolbar. Starting with the papaya on the right, select both the large and the small graphical elements: Command-click/Ctrl-click the OFF papaya layer and Command-Shift-click/Ctrl-Shift-click the ON papaya layer on the Layers palette.

3 Choose Create Slice from Selection from the Slices menu, and then click on the Rollover palette, where your slice appears as the first, or Normal, state.

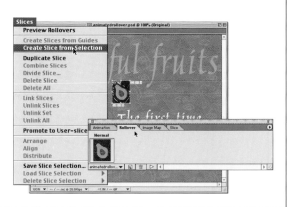

RELATED TIPS:

Animating GIFs, page 66
Creating Remote Rollovers, page 80

4 Click on the Creates new rollover state button at the bottom of the Rollover palette to create an Over state, and then toggle off visibility of the large papaya layer on the Layers palette. Now when someone rolls the mouse cursor over the papaya in the browser, the small papaya will appear.

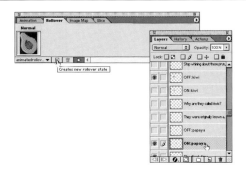

5 Now we'll create a second rollover state that triggers an animation (a fade) when the visitor clicks on the small papaya. Click the Creates New Rollover State button again and then change the type of rollover to Click by choosing it from the Selects Rollover State pop-up menu.

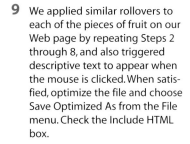

6 Go to the Animation palette and click the Duplicates Current Frame button at the bottom of the palette. We're going to have ImageReady "tween," or automatically create the intermediate frames of the animation, but first we need to set the final opacity of the papaya in this frame: change the Opacity of the small (on) papaya layer on the Layers palette to 20%.

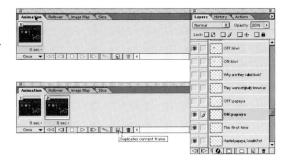

7 Shift-click to select the first and last frames of the animation, and then click the Tweens Animation Frames button at the bottom of the palette. In the Tween dialog box, specify the options for the animation. We chose All Layers so that all of the image will be visible, not just the papaya; we checked Opacity under Parameters; and we instructed ImageReady to create four intermediate frames. Click OK and you'll see all six frames appear.

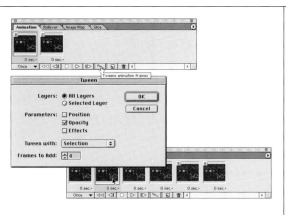

8 We finessed animation by changing the delay to .5 seconds for each frame and instructing it to loop once. You can preview the animation by clicking the Play button on the Animation palette, and test the rollover by clicking the Preview Rollover Behavior button on the Rollover palette. See your work in a browser at any time by choosing File > Preview In and selecting your preferred browser.

9 We applied similar rollovers to each of the pieces of fruit on our Web page by repeating Steps 2 through 8, and also triggered descriptive text to appear when the mouse is clicked. When satisfied, optimize the file and choose Save Optimized As from the File menu. Check the Include HTML box.

Creating Remote Rollovers

Once you get the hang of designing mouse rollovers, you can experiment with more advanced techniques. For example, you can construct a "remote" rollover — one in which a linked element on the page, such as text or a graphic, triggers the rollover effect but doesn't actually change state; instead, an image or text elsewhere on the page changes state. This creates a more dynamic and engaging experience for site visitors. To illustrate the concept, we've created a music site with CD titles along the right column. When a viewer rolls the mouse cursor over a title, an associated thumbnail appears in the center of the page (this is called the target), which in turn provides a link to a page with more information. We set up our example in GoLive by placing an image used as the background in an HTML document and laying an HTML table over it for the text and thumbnails.

1 Using Layout view in GoLive, drag to select the text that will trigger the first rollover effect. In our example, it's "1. cherubs crossing." On the Link tab of the Inspector, click the Create Link button.

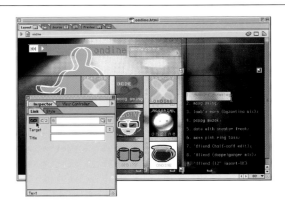

2 Click to select the "target"—the element that will change state when a viewer rolls the mouse cursor over the trigger. In our example, the target is the cherubs CD thumbnail graphic. Click the More tab in the Inspector and type a name for this image.

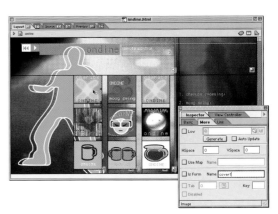

3 In the Basic tab of the Inspector, note the width and height of your on-state image in the target; it's 91 x 91 pixels in our example. In the Source field, browse to select the file that will be your off-state element. In our example, it's spacer.gif, a 1-x-1-pixel transparent image that is scaled by the browser to force the desired spacing, which lets the page background appear in the off state. Type in the on-state graphic's width and height.

RELATED TIPS:
Animating Rollovers, page 78

4 In the Layout window, you'll see the off-state target image (the spacer GIF that reveals the page background) has replaced the on-state CD thumbnail.

5 Click the trigger text again, and in the Events list of the Actions palette, select Mouse Enter to trigger the action that will happen when a mouse pointer is moved over the text. Then click the Create New Action button, and an action placeholder appears called None. In the Action pop-up menu, select Image > Set Image URL.

6 Click the Image pull-down menu and choose your target image, "cover1" in our example. In the Link field, browse to select the image that is the on state of the rollover, the cherubs CD cover, "images/cover/1.jpg," in our example.

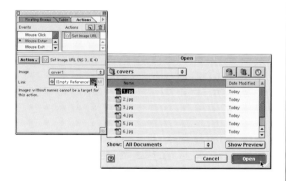

7 Finish the action by selecting Mouse Exit from the Events list of the Actions palette, clicking the Create New Action button, and selecting Image > Set Image URL from the Action pop-up menu. Choose the target image's off state for the Link field (in this example, spacer.gif) so that when the pointer is moved away from the trigger link, the target image returns to its normal state.

8 To add a hyperlink to the trigger element, select it in the Layout window, click the Link tab of the Inspector, and enter the URL. In our example, positioning the mouse over the trigger not only pops up a thumbnail of the CD cover on the page, but also lets the visitor jump to a linked page that displays information about the CD.

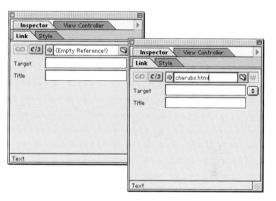

9 Repeat this process for any other remote rollovers you want to create. You can preview remote JavaScript rollovers in a browser at any time by clicking the Show in Browser button on the toolbar.

Designing Time-Independent Animations

One of LiveMotion's advanced features is time-independent animations. These animations, also called nested or character animations, play independently of the composition's main animation. They're great for rollover effects, because they can be triggered by a visitor action such as a mouse click, and they can also be used to create multiple animations on a page, such as when you want a logo to rotate continuously after the main animation finishes. Here's how to create time-independent animations in a LiveMotion composition in which three arrows move diagonally up and across the background, changing size as they go, while at the same time a cluster of smaller arrows and dots pulses in the corner of the page.

1 Start by creating the image for the composition in Photoshop. Elements that will be animated should be on their own layer; everything that will remain static resides on a background layer. In our example, the three arrows reside on three layers and the small dots on a fourth layer; all will be animated in LiveMotion. Save as a layered Photoshop file.

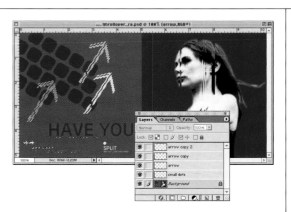

2 Launch LiveMotion and choose File > New. Create a new composition whose dimensions are the same as your Photoshop file, in this case 737 x 373 pixels. Specify a Frame Rate of 12, choose Auto-Layout from the Export pop-up menu, and check the Make HTML box.

3 Choose File > Place and place the Photoshop file you created in Step 1. LiveMotion imports the file as a single object. Choose Window > Timeline to view the artwork as the only object in your composition's timeline.

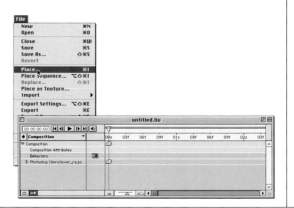

RELATED TIPS:
Creating Complex Animations, page 68
Importing Artwork for Animation, page 72
Creating Advanced Interactivity, page 86

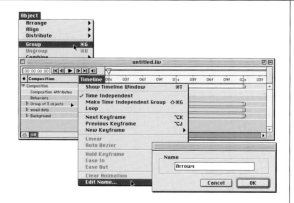

4 To access and animate the contents of your Photoshop layers, select the artwork in the timeline and choose Object > Convert Layers Into > Objects.

7 Hold down the Shift key while clicking the three arrow objects in the timeline to select them; then group them by choosing Object > Group. Give this object a more intuitive name, such as Arrows, in our example.

5 The composition window now displays bounding boxes around the objects that were layered in your Photoshop file, and the timeline shows those objects with the same names as your Photoshop layers.

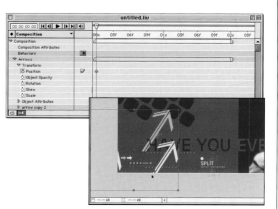

8 Toggle open the arrows' Transform attributes. With the current time marker set at 0 seconds, click the stopwatch icon next to Position for the arrows to set a starting keyframe. Then drag the arrows off the left side of the composition with the Selection tool.

6 The first animation we'll create will belong to the entire composition: It consists of the three arrows coming in from the left side of the background and moving diagonally across, up, and off the top of the page. To begin, select Composition in the timeline and drag the duration bar slider to the ending point of the animation, 2 seconds in our example.

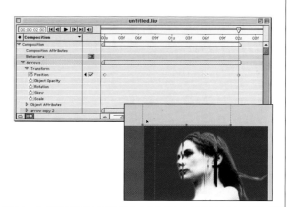

9 With the arrows still selected in the timeline, drag the current time marker to 2 seconds, check the box next to their Position attribute to set an ending keyframe, and drag the arrows off the top of the image.

Designing Time-Independent Animations

10 With Composition selected, click the Loop button at the bottom of the timeline. Then click the Preview button in the toolbar and watch the arrows move across the composition as directed.

11 Now we'll enhance this animation independently of the composition so that the arrows change size as they move across the composition the first time, but not on subsequent loops. To do this, we have to create an independent timeline by selecting the arrows object and then choosing Timeline > Time Independent. LiveMotion adds an icon next to the arrows in the timeline indicating that the object has an independent timeline.

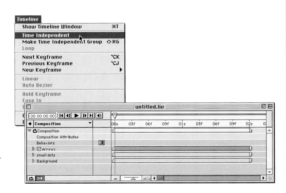

12 Now we'll make the arrows change size asynchronously. Double-click the Arrows object to open its timeline. Drag the duration bar slider to the end point of the animation (2 seconds in our example) if it's not already there; we want this animation to be the same length as the composition's.

13 With the current time marker at 0, select one of the group's objects, "arrow copy 2" in our example. The arrows are bounded by a blue box in the composition; the arrow we selected has handles on it so it can be transformed (you'll have to temporarily move the objects into the composition window to see this). Open its Transform attributes and click the stopwatch icon to set a Scale keyframe.

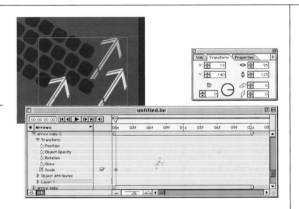

14 Move the current time marker to frame 6 and click on the check box to set a second scale keyframe. Then click on the bottom-right handle of the arrow and Shift-drag to proportionally scale the arrow to a new size, or enter new dimensions in the width and height fields of the Transform palette.

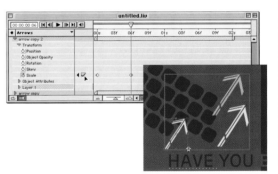

15 Move the current time marker to 1 second, set a third keyframe, and in the Transform palette reset the object to 100% of its original size (width: 95, height: 125). To repeat this transform for the second half of the animation, Shift-click on the frame 6 and 1-second keyframes and Option/Alt-drag them along the timeline to 1 frame 6 seconds and 2 seconds.

RELATED TIPS:
Creating Complex Animations, page 68
Importing Artwork for Animation, page 72
Creating Advanced Interactivity, page 86

16 Repeat Steps 13 through 15 for the remaining arrows, scaling to different sizes for variety.

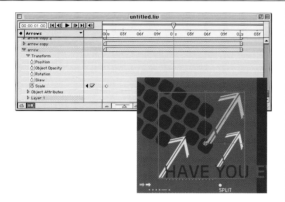

17 Return to the main composition timeline by clicking on the timeline name pop-up menu or on the navigator button, and click the Preview Mode button to watch your two animations. The arrows will cross the composition repeatedly, as instructed by the main composition animation, but they'll only change size on the first round, as instructed by the independent animation.

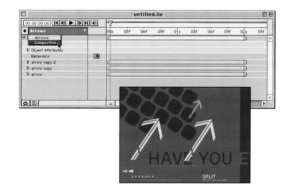

18 Now we'll animate the dots on the bottom of the composition so that they pulsate independently of the arrows' movement (the main composition animation). Select the small dots object in the timeline and choose Timeline > Time Independent.

19 Double-click the small dots object to open its timeline, toggle open its Object Attributes, and click the stopwatch to create a keyframe at 0 seconds for Replace. This action automatically creates two additional attributes that appear now in the timeline: Crop and Shape Resize. We unchecked the keyframes for Replace and Crop, leaving one only for Shape Resize, which is all we want to modify.

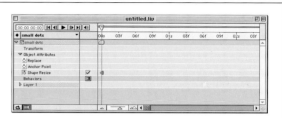

20 Drag the small dots' duration bar slider to frame 3, and then, as in Steps 14 and 15, insert keyframes at frames 1, 2, and 3, dragging the object's handles in the composition window to set it at varying sizes at each keyframe. Set this animation to loop by clicking on the Loop button at the bottom of the timeline; this way it will loop for the length of the composition and continually thereafter, since the composition itself is also set to loop.

21 In addition to previewing your final animation in LiveMotion, be sure to test it in a browser. Choose File > Preview In and select a browser from those on your computer.

ARTWORK: Renee Anderson

simplify.com

unique housewares for your simple lifestyle

| locations | about | products | contact us |

With LiveMotion, you're not merely limited to creating visual effects: You can also create a multisensory experience using sound, and you can enhance interactive experiences with behaviors. Sound clips are often used to accompany a site splash screen—drum roll, please—or so that visitors hear a "click" when they click on a button. LiveMotion's behaviors can make things happen on a Web page when a visitor interacts with an object; they play animations, for example, or link to other Web pages. This technique shows you how to add sound to a navigational button and trigger an animation to play during a rollover. As usual, we started with a comp created in Photoshop, but you can also execute the technique using objects that you draw in LiveMotion. Be sure to preview your animation frequently so that you can refine each effect as you go, and remember to test your results in multiple browsers before saving and exporting the final piece to an HTML authoring program.

1 Create your comp in Photoshop, with each element you want to animate residing on its own layer. Here, clouds with descriptive text fade in when triggered by a rollover. Each cloud layer consists of a cloud form and related text, all flattened onto one layer. Keep the text for the four navigational buttons on separate layers as well, with the rest of the comp as the background. We'll create the actual buttons in Live-Motion. Save your image as a layered Photoshop file.

2 Launch LiveMotion and choose File > New. Create a new composition whose dimensions are the same as your Photoshop file, 720 x 474 pixels in our example. Use the other default settings and click OK. Then choose Place from the File menu to place the Photoshop file you created in Step 1.

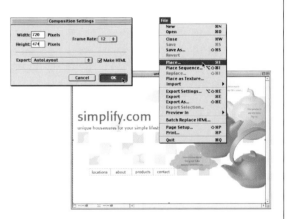

3 Go to the Timeline > Show Timeline Window and you will see the name of your Photoshop file. In order to animate the contents of your Photoshop layers later, click on the placed artwork in the Timeline and choose Object > Convert Layers Into > Objects. After the conversion of your layers into objects, you can easily see in the Timeline Window how all the layer names from your PSD file have been preserved for each object.

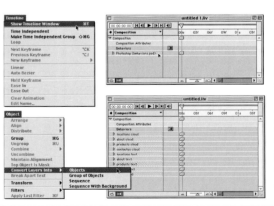

RELATED TIPS:

Creating Remote Rollovers, page 80
Designing Time-Independent Animations, page 82

Adobe Photoshop 6.0   Adobe LiveMotion 1.0

4 Since we didn't create the button shapes in Photoshop, as we did the button's outlines and text labels, we will use LiveMotion's Rectangle tool to draw white shapes for each button inside the purple outlines. Use the Object > Arrange > Bring Forward command to ensure that your labels appear in front of your buttons. Bring the Timeline window to the front and use the Timeline > Edit Name command to give each object an intuitive name, using a systematic naming convention.

5 Select the first navigational button shape for which you want to create a rollover effect, locations BUTTON in our example, and view its "normal" state in the Rollovers palette by choosing Window > Rollovers.

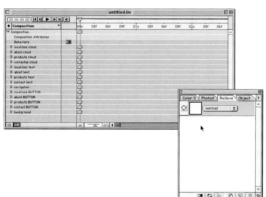

6 Click the New Rollover State button three times to create "over," "down," and "out" states for the Locations button. Notice in the timeline that creating additional rollover states automatically generates an independent timeline for the button. We'll use it later; first we'll define the rollover states.

7 First we want the button to change color when the mouse cursor is positioned over it, so select its over state in the Rollovers palette. We could use the Color palette to choose a color, but we want to use one from the composition, so with the Eyedropper tool we choose a light green from one of our teapots. The button reflects this change in the composition window.

8 We also want the button to become a darker color when a visitor clicks it, so we select its down state in the Rollovers palette and use the Eyedropper again to choose a darker green from the same the teapot.

9 Now we'll add sound to the rollover. Choose Window > Sounds to open the Sounds palette, select various sounds, and click Play to hear them. Then, with the over state selected, choose the sound that you want associated with it ("Ting" in our example) and click the Apply button at the bottom of the Sounds palette. Then apply a different sound to the down rollover state (we used "Chime Glint").

10 Now we want to add a "remote" element to this rollover—fade in a cloud of steam with explanatory text above a teapot when the mouse rolls over the Locations button. Since the cloud will be associated with a rollover state, we have to make it time independent. So select the Locations Cloud objects in the timeline and choose Timeline > Make Time Independent Group.

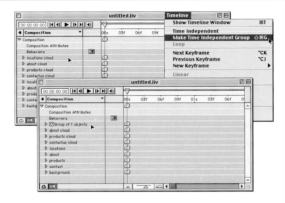

11 Choose Timeline > Edit Name to give "Group of 1 objects" an intuitive name, "locationsGroup" in our example, and then double-click it to access its independent timeline. Drag its right (ending) duration bar slider to 1 second; that's when the cloud and its text will be completely faded in.

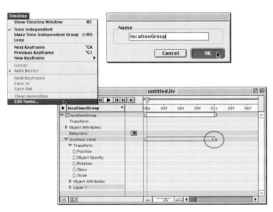

12 Toggle open the Transform attributes for the locations cloud shape and text. With the current time marker at frame 1, click the stopwatch icon next to the cloud's Object Opacity attribute to create a starting keyframe for the fade; LiveMotion automatically creates one for the text, too. In the Opacity palette, drag the Object Opacity slider to zero.

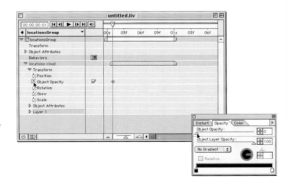

13 Drag the current time marker to the end of the animation, 1 second in our example. Check the box next to the location cloud's Object Opacity attribute to create an ending keyframe, and then drag the Object Opacity slider to 100 in the Opacity palette.

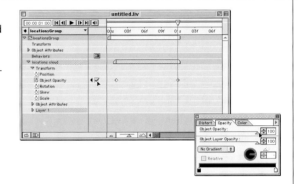

14 Now we'll make sure that the locations cloud and text appear when they're supposed to. First, drag the left (starting) duration bar slider to frame 1 for the locations cloud object.

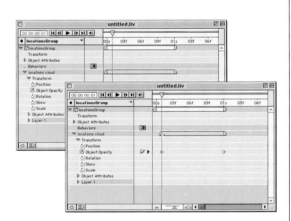

15 Then position the current time marker at 0 seconds and click on the Behavior button. In the Edit Behaviors dialog box that appears, label your behavior "locations-STOP" and choose Stop from the Add Behavior pop-up menu. In the Options area, select "locationsGroup" as your Target. Click OK.

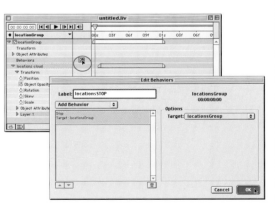

RELATED TIPS:

Creating Remote Rollovers, page 80
Designing Time-Independent Animations, page 82

16 Drag the current time marker to frame 1 and click the Behaviors button again. In the Edit Behaviors dialog box, label this behavior "locationsPLAY" and choose Play from the Add Behavior pop-up menu. Again, your target is "locationsGroup." Click OK. These two Behaviors instruct the animation to refrain from playing until frame 1.

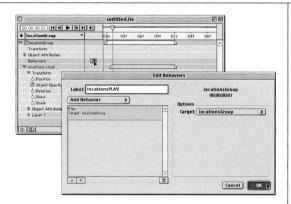

17 Still, we have to trigger the animation to play at that time by associating it with a button rollover state. To do this, go to back to the Composition timeline by using the Active Timeline pulldown menu and then double-click the locations button to access its independent timeline.

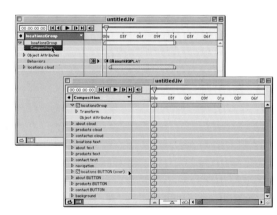

18 Select the button's over state in the Rollovers palette, and click on the Edit Behaviors button at the bottom of the palette. In the resulting dialog box, select Play from the Add Behavior menu and select "locationsGroup" from the Target menu. Click OK.

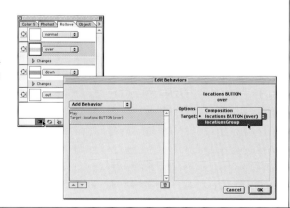

19 Now select the button's out state from the Rollovers palette and click the Edit Behaviors button again. Select Go to Label from the Add Behavior menu, and choose "locationsGroup" as the Target and "locationsSTOP" as the Label. Then, before closing the dialog box, select Go to Label again from the Add Behavior menu, choose "locationsGroup" as the Target, and then choose "Play Cloud" for the Label. Click OK.

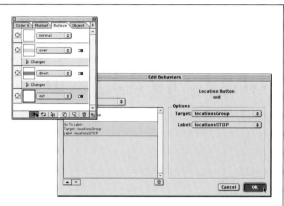

20 Finally, we want to link the locations button to a URL address. To do this, select its down state in the Rollovers palette and then click the Edit Behaviors button. In the Edit Behaviors dialog box, choose Go to URL from the Add Behavior menu, and type the desired URL in the text box in the Options area. Choose _blank from the Frame pop-up to make the page open in a new browser window. Click OK.

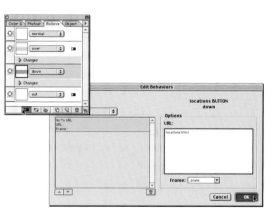

21 Repeat Steps 5 through 20 for each of the remaining buttons in the composition, applying the same color and sound effects for their over and down rollover states, but triggering different steam clouds to fade in and adding the appropriate URL links.

Management Techniques

Using Actions to Automate Tasks

Many Adobe applications let you group a series of commands into what it calls actions, which automate such routine production tasks as applying text or an effect to a series of navigational buttons. Photoshop, ImageReady, and Illustrator all feature an Actions palette where the commands can be recorded; and all three applications ship with a number of prerecorded actions, such as creating a vignette, creating a rollover state, and saving a file for the Web. Here we show you how we created an action using Photoshop to save navigation buttons for a prototype online game site. You can also execute this technique in Illustrator or ImageReady. We've noted in parentheses when the steps to follow for these programs differ from what's been described.

1 Create your original button templates as Photoshop files that contain individual layers for text and shapes. Use a Web-safe palette and save them as 8-bit RGB in a "button templates" folder.

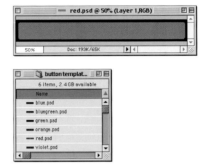

2 On the Actions palette, choose New Set from the pop-up menu, or click on the folder icon at the bottom of the palette. Our set is named "riot buttons." (If you're using ImageReady, skip this step and go to Step 3.)

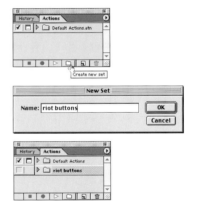

3 Choose New Action from the pop-up menu and give the action a logical name, such as "riotbutton-action." Assign a function key if you like. Click the Record button to begin recording the steps of the task you want to automate. The action appears in your set on the palette.

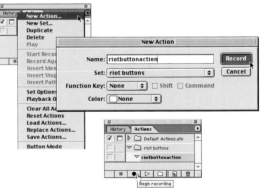

RELATED TIPS:

Automating Tasks with Droplets, page 96

4 Open your first button file, Option/Alt double-click on the shape layer to open the Layer Properties dialog box, and change the layer name to "button."

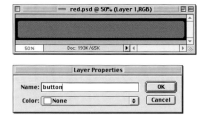

5 The Actions palette records the name change as the first step of your action.

6 Select the Type tool, click on your image, and enter the text you want for the button in your image. Specify the color and other settings in the options bar. When you're satisfied, lock in the text by clicking the checkmark button on the options bar. (In Illustrator, you don't have to lock in the changes.)

7 Photoshop automatically puts the text on its own layer and names it according to the words you typed. To keep things simple, Option/Alt double-click on the type layer to bring up the Layer Properties dialog box and change the name to "text."

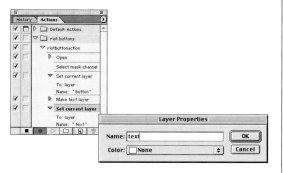

8 To center the text on the button, select the button layer and click the link box on the text layer to link the two layers together. Then choose Align Linked from the Layer menu and choose Vertical Centers. Repeat the Align Linked command choosing Horizontal Centers. (In Illustrator, select the objects and use the Align palette.)

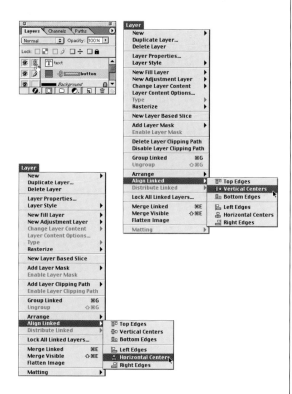

8 If the type doesn't look perfectly centered, nudge it by unlinking the layers and then selecting only the text layer. With the Move tool, use the arrow keys to precisely center the text in the button.

9 When you're satisfied, make the finished button a GIF by choosing Save for Web from the File menu. (Use the Optimize palette in Image-Ready.) We applied a Perceptual palette, no dither, and 8 colors. Because you designed the template using only a few Web-safe colors, you can keep the file size small. Click OK, and then create a folder to store the new GIFs, name your finished button, and save it.

10 Close the image and choose Don't Save in the warning box, because you'll use this button template again. This is the last step in your action, so click the Stop recording button (the one with the black square at the bottom left of the Actions palette).

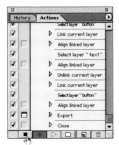

11 You're not done yet! At this point, the action will open the same button, type the same text, and save a GIF with the same name. To automatically open certain dialog boxes as you play the action, you need to select the Toggle dialog on/off icons on the Actions palette.

94

RELATED TIPS:

Automating Tasks with Droplets, page 96

12 Toggle on the following dialog boxes: Open, so that you can select a button; Make Text Layer, so that you can enter the text that appears on the button; and Export, so that you can save your final button with a new name. In our case, the nudging we performed for the first button looked good on all of our buttons, but you can also toggle that step on and manually nudge the text for each button.

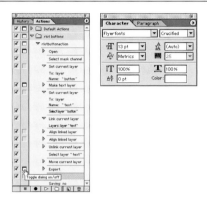

13 Now you can execute the action by selecting it and then clicking the play button at the bottom of the Actions palette. Photoshop prompts you to open the next button file so that it can perform the tasks you recorded.

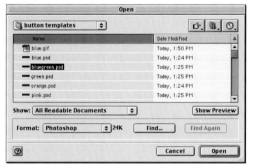

14 Your new files are saved in a folder, ready to be placed in an HTML page in GoLive.

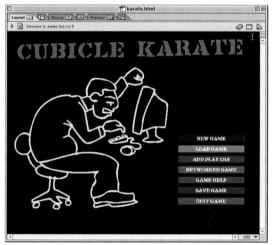

Using Droplets to Automate Tasks

ARTWORK: Zanne deJanvier

In addition to actions, Adobe offers a nifty little production feature called droplets, which let you batch-process images by dragging and dropping them onto an icon. Batch processing can't be beat when you want to steamline the preparation of navigational and other kinds of graphics that require systematic, uniform editing or optimization. Droplets are based on actions, and although they used to be available only in ImageReady, now they're in Photoshop, too (but not Illustrator). Here we show you how we took a collection of scanned watercolor paintings and used an action and a droplet in ImageReady to automate the process of making them a consistent quality and size. A limited version of this technique can be executed in Photoshop, as noted in the steps.

1 Open one of the scanned images, a Photoshop file in this example, and use it to define your droplet. Don't create a new image, because an empty document won't let you see if your scaling works properly.

2 First we will create an action, and then we'll create a droplet based on the action. To create the action, choose New Action from the Actions palette pop-up menu (or click the button at the bottom of the palette), name your action, and click the Begin Recording button. The new action appears on the Actions palette.

3 Choose Adjust from the Image menu, then choose Levels. Adjust the sliders until you're satisfied with the changes made to the image, and then click OK. Repeat for any other color adjustments you might want to make, such as changing brightness and contrast. Note that each operation appears as a step in your action.

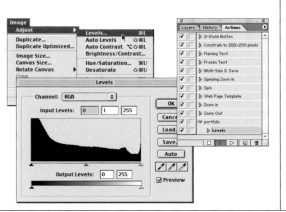

96

RELATED TIPS:
Using Actions to Automate Tasks, page 92

Adobe ImageReady 3.0   Adobe Photoshop 6.0

4 Choose Image Size from the Image menu and specify your desired maximum height—300 pixels in this example. Since the width of the original scanned images may vary, constrain proportions only by height. Check the Action Options box and then opt to fit the image by width and check the Do Not Enlarge box, because you don't want the quality of the art to be compromised by being enlarged too much.

5 Click on the Optimized tab of your image window to preview the image as you save it for the Web. On the Optimize palette, choose GIF as your file format and use a Perceptual palette with, say, 32 colors and a Diffusion dither of 100%. There's no transparency in this image, so the Transparency and Matte options don't apply.

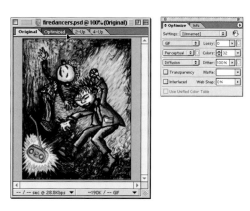

6 Choose Save Optimized As from the File menu, check Save Images, and click the Save button to save your new GIF in a folder called Images. Then click the Stop Recording button at the bottom of the Actions palette and close your image without saving it.

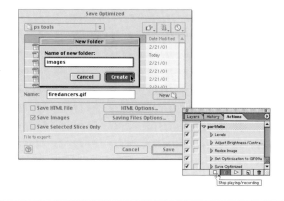

7 Now begin creating your droplet. Drag the action to the desktop to save it as an executable droplet, or chose Create Droplet from the Actions palette pop-up menu. You'll see the droplet icon on your desktop. (In Photoshop, choose File > Automate > Create Droplet.)

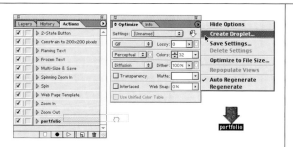

8 Now you can drag your group of scanned images onto the droplet and they will be automatically adjusted and resized (in Photoshop) as well as optimized and saved as a GIF (in Image-Ready) into the same folder as the one in which they already reside. Meanwhile, you can go get a cup of coffee!

9 To streamline the optimization of a series of graphic files, use the Create Droplet icon in the Optimize palette. With any image open, specify the palette, colors, and other settings that you want to use, and then click the downward-arrow icon to save the settings as a droplet. Then drag the folder containing your images onto the droplet to automatically optimize them. They'll be saved in the same folder as the originals.

Using Layer Sets to Manage Files

Web design is a collaborative process. You often find yourself working with Photoshop files created by other designers, and after you've done your magic—say, to create a comp of a home page—you then have to hand off the files to someone else. Under these circumstances, it's easy for Photoshop files to devolve into chaos: Files may have 50 layers, give or take a dozen, without clear labels or a discernible order. Luckily, Photoshop has a lot of great tools, such as layer sets, for reining in such chaos. Here's how to systematically manage layers and save your peers and clients from wasting valuable hours stumbling around in your Photoshop files.

1 Decide how you want your Web page organized. For PCWorld Online (www.pcworld.com), we divided the page into the following 9 sections: One template for the logo and navigational system; one template for the elements that remain constant throughout the site (the background, left and right columns); and the seven topic sections (Home, News, Reviews, Here's How, Features, Downloads, and Channels).

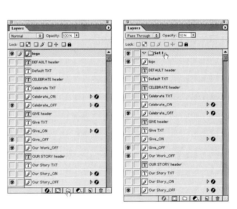

2 With this organization in mind, make layer sets accordingly. Click on the Create a New Set button at the bottom of the Layers palette (the folder icon). A default folder named "Set1" appears.

3 Assign properties to the layer set: Select Layer Set Properties from the Layers palette's pop-up menu and give your set a name (such as "Logo:Template") and a color.

4 To place a layer into the folder, simply click to select it and drag it onto the folder. Photoshop assigns it the appropriate color.

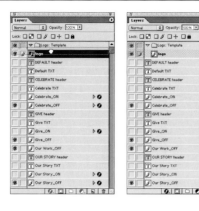

5 You can organize layer sets any way you please by dragging to position, or "stack," set folders on the Layers palette. We stacked the folders according to where their content appears on the canvas. In other words, we worked from top to bottom, left to right, listing the folders accordingly: logo, Home, News, Reviews, and so on, with the background last, or at the bottom of the list on the palette.

6 You can also drag to stack layers within folders in whatever order you desire. We positioned "on" rollover state layers directly above corresponding "off" state layers.

7 If you want to rename a layer at any time, perhaps to clarify "on" as "on state," simply click to select the layer and choose Layer Properties from the Layers palette's pop-up menu. You can make your change in the dialog box that appears.

8 Delete unwanted layers at any time by clicking on them and dragging them to the Trash at the bottom of the Layers palette.

Using PDFs to Proof Comps

ARTWORK: Julia Hummelt

Acrobat is a great tool for reviewing Web pages, especially when the design and client teams are at different locations. After pages or sites have been comped in HTML, you can use Acrobat's Web Capture command to bring HTML documents into PDF format, maintaining formatting, text, images, colors, and links. Then you can e-mail the PDF to reviewers, who can mark up the pages offline using Acrobat's annotation tools. This is much easier than trying to give everyone access to live HTML, or having people view pages independently and write up comments in a hodge-podge of documents. The designer receives PDFs that accurately reflect the page design, with feedback that can be easily synthesized for a new draft. It's also a great way for Web administrators to archive sites, and for designers to create portable portfolios.

1 Before you download and convert a Web page to PDF, specify your Web Capture options. Choose Open Web Page from the File menu in Acrobat and click on the Conversion Settings button in the Open Web Page dialog box.

2 On the General tab of the Conversion Settings dialog box, check Create Bookmarks to New Content to create bookmarks for each downloaded Web page, which will help you organize and navigate your captured pages. You can also select the HTML file description, click on the Settings button, and specify how you want HTML layouts and fonts to be converted.

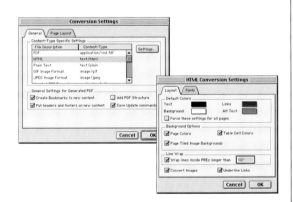

3 On the Page Layout tab, you can specify the PDF page attributes so that they can be viewed and printed easily. Pages with lots of scrollable vertical content should be in portrait mode.

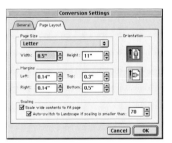

4 Now prepare your HTML page for capture. Open it in GoLive and click on the Preview In button to view it in a browser of your choice. To proof your site, post the page or pages to your internal server and view the top-level page in the browser. If you only want a particular page, post that page and view it in the browser.

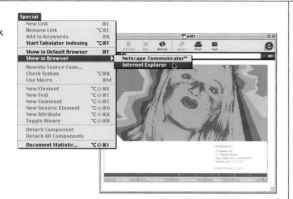

5 In the browser, drag to select the URL. Press Command-C/Ctrl-C to copy it.

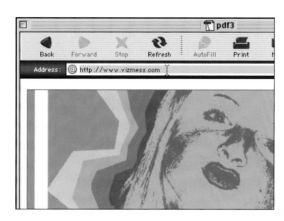

6 Switch to Acrobat. If the dialog box isn't still open, choose File > Open Web Page, and then press Command-V/Ctrl-V and paste the URL into the text box. If you want to capture an entire site, click the Get Entire Site button; if you want the opening page plus those it links to, check the Levels button and specify 2. Then click Download.

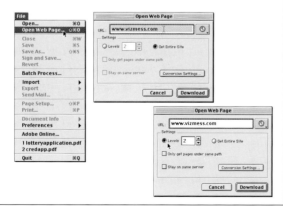

7 Your Web page appears as a PDF file in Acrobat, with the Bookmarks palette displayed on the left. Click on the bookmarks to navigate through the file. Move the cursor over links to see their URLs; click to download them if they're not already part of the PDF document, or to jump to that PDF page if they are.

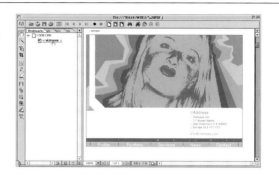

8 Choose Save As from the File menu to save the file with an intuitive name (instead of URL.pdf).

9 Now you or anyone with whom you share the file can mark up desired changes using Acrobat's annotation tools. For example, draw with the Notes tool to add a comment; circle problematic graphics with the Pencil tool; select text with the Highlight tool; or use the Strikethrough tool to delete text. Double-click on any drawn annotation for a pop-up window where you can write a message. Click with the Stamp tool if everything is fine.

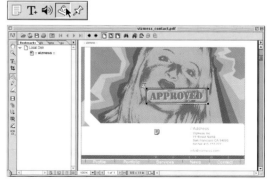

Reference

Chapter 6

Understanding Color Palettes

ARTWORK: Dohyun Kim

GIF images support up to 256 colors, so whenever you optimize GIF graphics for the Web, you have a choice of several color reduction algorithms, also called palettes or color tables, to bring your images down to a range supported by the GIF format. The trick, of course, is to choose an algorithm that preserves image quality while reducing the size of the file to the greatest extent possible. In Photoshop and Illustrator, you optimize GIFs and access the color palette of your choice in the Save for Web dialog box; in ImageReady, you use the Optimize palette. Here we walk you through each of your color palette options, explaining their strengths and showing how they render colors differently.

1 The Adaptive palette samples the colors that most commonly appear in the image. This preserves image integrity at the expense of Web-safe colors. If your image has one or two predominant colors—for example, greens and blues—and you want a palette that favors those hues, choose Adaptive. For an even more precise palette, select a part of your image that contains the colors you want to emphasize and then optimize the image.

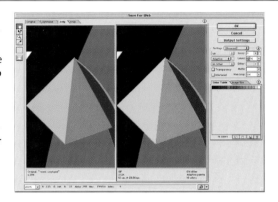

2 The Perceptual palette creates a color table based on the colors that are the most sensitive to the human eye; the brightest colors in the image are used in the Perceptual palette.

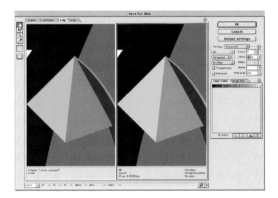

3 The Selective palette is similar to the Perceptual palette but it favors darker areas of an image. Both the Perceptual and Selective palettes emphasize the yellow part of the spectrum, but Selective preserves Web-safe colors better than the Perceptual or Adaptive palette. According to Adobe, Selective produces images with the greatest color integrity.

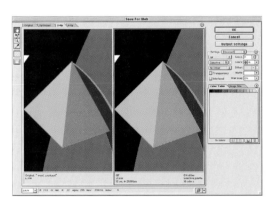

4 The Web palette adheres to the 216 colors that Web browsers use to display images on 256-color monitors. It generally produces images with the worst color integrity. However, it's a good idea to use it when you don't want browsers to dither the image on 256-color monitors.

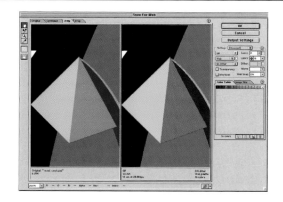

5 The Windows palette uses Windows' default 256-color palette, which is based on a uniform sampling of RGB colors. If your image contains fewer than 256 colors, the unused colors are removed from the palette. You may want to use this palette, for example, if your company's Intranet site runs only on Windows machines.

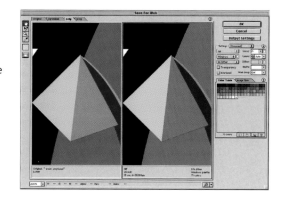

6 The Mac OS palette uses the default Mac OS 8-bit palette, which, like the Windows palette, is based on a uniform sampling of RGB colors. If your image contains fewer than 256 colors, the unused colors are removed from the palette. Like the Windows palette, you may want to use this palette if you know your audience is viewing the art only on Macintosh computers.

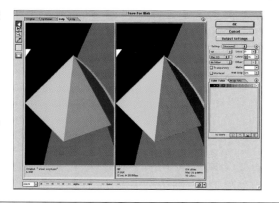

7 On rare occasions you might want to use the Black & White or Grayscale color reduction algorithms, which remove color from the image and apply a black and white or grayscale palette, just as you would expect.

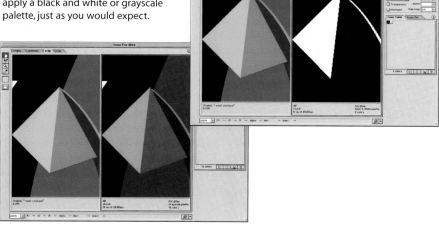

Creating a Master Palette

When you have multiple images that must display the same colors or when you need to share the colors with co-workers, make a custom master palette. Create an image in Illustrator or Photoshop that contains the colors you want in the palette—preferably Web-safe colors— and then open it in ImageReady and choose Image > Master Palette > Add to Master Palette (or choose Clear Master Palette first, if it's prompted). In the Optimize palette, apply a color reduction algorithm and other settings for your GIF, then choose Image > Master Palette > Build Master Palette to create the color table; finally, choose Image > Master Palette > Save Master Palette. The palette, which has an .act file extension, should reside in Adobe Photoshop > Presets > Optimized Colors. Then it will be available from the color reduction algorithm pop-up menu for other GIFs and PNG-8 files. To view the colors in your master palette, choose the master palette from the menu and look at the Color Table.

Understanding Blending Modes

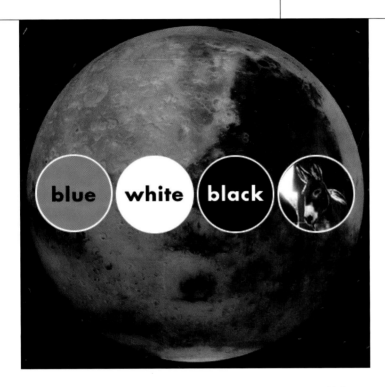

Photoshop offers more than a dozen blending modes, each specifying a unique way that pixels of different colors interact. You can apply a blending mode using a variety of tools, including the Paintbrush, Gradient, and Airbrush tools; or by specifying a mode on the Layers palette or in the New Layers dialog box. The results of these effects are relatively easy to foresee when mixing two flat colors, but when blending a solid color with an underlying photograph or texture, the results are less predictable. Although the best way to learn the effects of blending is simply to experiment, here we provide a starting point by demonstrating some of the effects you get when blending a layer of solid colors with a photograph on an underlying layer.

1 Multiply always produces a darker color than the original (at left). Painting with black produces black; painting with white leaves the original color unchanged.

2 Screen is the inverse of Multiply: Painting in Screen mode always produces a lighter color, unless you paint with black, which leaves the original color unchanged.

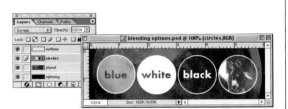

3 Overlay preserves the highlights and shadows of the original color because the original color is mixed with the paint color, not replaced by it.

4 Soft Light produces the effect of a diffuse spotlight: If the paint color is lighter than 50 percent gray, the image is lightened. If the paint color is darker than 50 percent gray, the image is darkened.

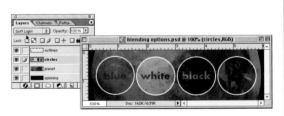

5 Hard Light operates like Soft Light mode, but it produces a harsher spotlight effect. Painting with pure black or white produces pure black or white, respectively.

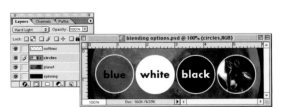

RELATED TIPS:
Creating Artwork with Transparency, page 22
Understanding Alpha Channels, page 110

6 Color Dodge brightens the original color to reflect the paint color. Painting with black doesn't change the color of the original pixels.

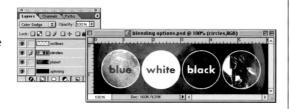

7 Color Burn is the inverse of Color Dodge: It darkens the original color to reflect the paint color. Painting with white leaves pixels unchanged.

8 Darken selects whichever is darker, the original or the paint color, and changes pixels to that color. Pixels darker than the paint color do not change.

9 Lighten selects whichever is lighter, the original or the paint color, and changes pixels to that color. Pixels lighter than the paint color do not change.

10 Difference subtracts the original color from the paint color or vice versa, depending on which is brighter. Blending with black leaves pixels unchanged; blending with white inverts the original pixels' color values.

11 Exclusion produces an effect similar to that produced by Difference mode but with less contrast.

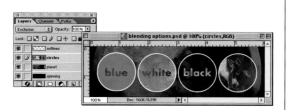

12 Hue produces a final color that has the hue of the paint color but the luminance and saturation of the original color.

13 Saturation produces a final color that has the saturation of the paint color but the luminance and hue of the original color.

14 Color produces a final color that has the luminance of the original color but the hue and saturation of the paint color. It is useful for colorizing or tinting monochrome images.

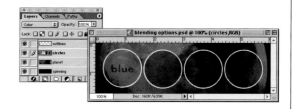

15 Luminosity produces a final color that has the luminance of the paint color but the hue and saturation of the original color.

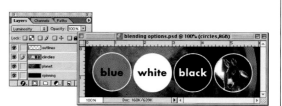

Understanding Channels

ARTWORK: Laura Dorothy Haertling

Every Photoshop image contains grayscale channels that store the image's color information (the channels correspond to CMYK, RGB, and LAB modes). The relationship between channels and layers can be confusing. We build complex images by placing different elements on separate layers, but all of the image's color data, regardless of layers, lives in channels. You can use the channels to control color in your image independently of layers. For instance, you can add spot channels for process-color printing, or you can use alpha channels to mask and optimize selected areas for print or Web publishing (see page 110 for more about alpha channels). Here we show you how to adjust the color of a multi-layered Photoshop image.

1 Open an image in Photoshop and choose Show Channels from the Window menu. If it is a CMYK document, you'll see a composite CMYK channel, plus individual channels for cyan, magenta, yellow, and black; if it's LAB you'll see a composite plus channels for luminance, and a and b color channels. Here we have an RGB image and its associated channels; the composite is selected by default, and all the colors are visible in the image.

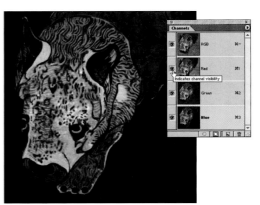

2 Toggle on the visibility of individual channels to see only the grayscale pixel information in your image. When you look at an individual channel, such as the blue channel in our example, both the thumbnail and the image display all of the pixels that contain blue values, which range from 0 brightness (black) to 255 brightness (white). (If you Shift-click to select multiple channels, the channels appear in color.)

3 Go to the Layers palette. Notice that all of your layers have been visible; thus, you have been seeing the blue pixels for all of the layers in your image. To see the blue pixels for the content of an individual layer, click the eye icons on individual layers until just one or two selected layers are visible. The image now displays the blue channel for those layers.

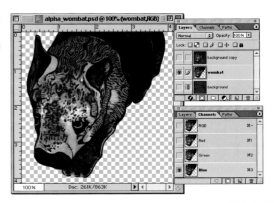

RELATED TIPS:

4 Now let's change the color of our friendly brown wombat and see what happens to our channel data. You can alter colors in an image in many ways; we will use Levels, which lets you adjust the tonal range and color balance of an image by changing the intensity of the image's shadows, midtones, and highlights. Choose Image > Adjust > Levels or press Command-L/Ctrl-L.

5 In the Levels dialog box, notice the Channels pop-up menu; you can make changes to an individual channel, multiple channels, or to the composite. To adjust multiple channels, select them in the Channels palette before calling up the Levels dialog box, the pop-up menu will reflect that.

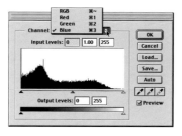

6 Since we want to make our wombat blue, we isolate the blue channel and maximize the blue data in our image by adjusting the histogram sliders: We moved the center arrow to the left to make the midtones more intense without changing the highlight or shadows in this channel.

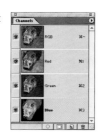
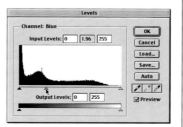

7 Voilà. The wombat is now blue.

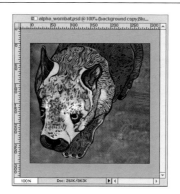

8 If you isolate the blue channel, you'll see the grayscale pixels reflect the change. Compare it to the original blue channel in Step 2.

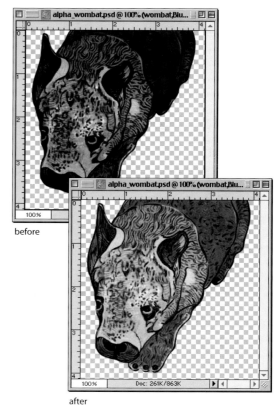

before

after

Understanding Alpha Channels

Alpha channels, which are selections saved as 8-bit grayscale "masks," are used to control the application of color edits or effects in an image. Once you save a selection as an alpha channel, Photoshop lets you either protect that masked area from color edits, filters, or other effects, or apply effects or edits to only the masked area. When you create complex or detailed selections, it's especially helpful to save them as alpha channels so that you can reuse them without having to manually re-create them. Alpha channels are particularly important to Web designers because they're the basis of Photoshop's and ImageReady's weighted optimization feature, which lets you vary optimization settings across an image to either produce gradual variations in GIF dithering or lossy settings, or control JPEG compression. Here is an overview of how to create and edit alpha channels.

1 To create an alpha channel from the content of a layer, Command-click/Ctrl-click the layer on the Layers palette. This selects the content of that layer; you'll see the marching ants selection boundary in the image window.

2 Click on the Channel tab and save the selection as a channel by clicking on the Save selection as channel button at the bottom of the Channels palette. You can, in fact, use this button to create a channel from any selection, including those created with the marquee, lasso, or Magic Wand tool.

3 Photoshop gives the channel a default name of Alpha 1 on the Channels palette. Make the alpha channel the only visible channel in the image. Photoshop displays selected pixels in white; unselected (masked) pixels in black, and partially transparent pixels in gray.

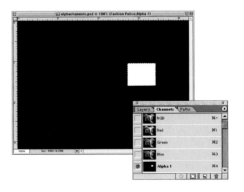

4 Now make all channels visible in the Channels palette. The alpha channel appears in full color with a marching ants boundary. The masked pixels appear with a semi-opaque red tint, much like a traditional rubylith overlay. Give the channel a more intuitive name by selecting it on the palette and choosing Channel Options from the palette's pop-up menu. You can also change the display settings, but the defaults suit us fine.

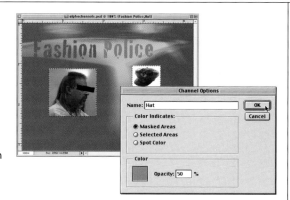

5 Edit the channel by painting in the image with a paint or editing tool: Paint with white to add to the channel; paint with black to subtract from it. Paint with a lower opacity to add or subtract semi-transparent pixels. The thumbnail in the Channels palette reflects your changes.

6 You can also change the contents of the alpha channel by making new selections: Make a selection in the image with a marquee tool or Command-click/Ctrl-click on a layer on the Layers palette. Choose Select > Save Selection. In the Save Selection dialog box, choose the alpha channel to which you want to add from the Channel pop-up menu and click the Add to Channel radio button. Now our hat channel also includes the vest.

7 What if you have created multiple alpha channels and want to combine them? First select the contents of one of the channels, "hat" in this example, by Command-clicking/ Ctrl-clicking it on the Channels palette.

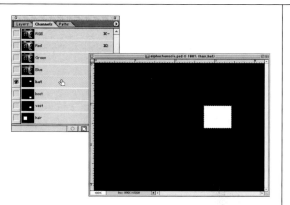

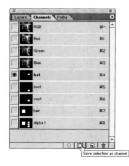

8 Then press Shift-Command/Shift-Ctrl while clicking on the channel or channels that you want to add to the first (boot, vest, and hair, in our example), and click the Save selection as channel button. A new channel contains the complete selection.

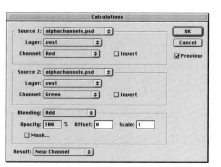

9 Another way to manage alpha channel contents is to use the Image > Calculations command. In the Calculations dialog box, choose the two desired source channels and select a Blending Mode from the pop-up list. You can choose Add or Subtract; control the opacity, offset, and scale of the calculation; specify whether and how to create a mask; and save the results as a document or a selection instead of as a channel.

Understanding Style Sheet Attributes

Inspector Tab	GoLive Attribute	Compatibility		Description	Issues
		Internet Explorer	Netscape Navigator		
Font	Color	3.0+	4.0+	Sets the font color.	
	Size	3.0+	4.0+	Sets the font size in absolute or relative terms.	Use pixels to ensure that text displays identically across all browsers or use ex, em, small, medium, large, smaller, larger, or relative to let visitors control font size within their browsers.
	Line Height	4.0+	4.0+	Sets the vertical space for a line of type, overriding browser settings. Also called line-spacing, leading, or ruling.	
	Font Family	3.0+	4.0+	Defines which fonts should be used in your order of preference.	
	Style	4.0+	4.0+	Sets the type as italic or roman.	Oblique is recognized by Explorer 4.0 but displayed as italic. Navigator 4.0 does not recognize oblique.
	Weight	4.0+	4.0+	Sets the type as bolder or lighter.	Most browsers support only normal and bold, so numeric attributes will be rounded to 400 or 700.
	Decoration	4.0+	4.0+	Adds underlining, strikethrough, and other formatting options.	Explorer v?? removed the "blink" attribute (as with the blink tag) because it is annoying.
Text	Text Indent	4.0+	4.0+	Indents the first line of text in a block.	
	Word Spacing	4.0+	6.0+	Controls the space between words.	Percentages do not work in any browser.
	Letter Spacing	4.0+	6.0+	Controls the space between characters in a word.	Percentages do not work in any browser.
	Vertical Align	4.0+	6.0+	Controls the vertical position of text on the line.	Explorer 4.0 recognizes only sub and super values.
	Font Variant	4.0+	6.0+	Makes lowercase letters small caps.	Explorer 4.0 does not make text smaller.
	Transformation	4.0+	4.0+	Makes letters in a line case consistent (all lower-, all upper-, or sentence case).	
	Alignment	4.0+	4.0+	Applies left, right, or justified alignment to text.	"Justify" stretches lines to full width of container. In some version 4.0 browsers, justify fails and text is left-aligned.
Block	Margin	4.0+	4.0+	Sets the margin around a block of text; allows negative values.	Is not included in an element's width and height. For example, a 400-pixel-wide element with a left margin of 20 pixels will be 420 pixels wide but have only 400 usable pixels.
	Padding	4.0+	4.0+	Defines the space inside of a block element's bounding box; must be a positive value.	Padding is included in the width and height of an element.
	Width	4.0+	4.0+	Sets the width of a block element's bounding box.	

RELATED TIPS:

Applying Style Sheets to HTML Pages, page 58
Specifying Fonts for Your Site, page 42

GoLive lets you define three kinds of styles: classes, which apply to individual blocks of text in an HTML document; tags, which apply to entire groups of HTML elements; and IDs, which can be applied to discrete paragraphs or ranges of text. Here's a guide to the style sheet attributes that GoLive supports, as they appear in the Inspector Tab (sometimes called properties).

Adobe GoLive 5.0

Inspector Tab	GoLive Attribute	Compatibility		Description	Issues
		Internet Explorer	Netscape Navigator		
Block	Height	4.0+	4.0+	Sets the height of a block element's bounding box.	
	Float	4.0+	4.0+	Allows text to wrap around an element.	Due to differences between browsers, this should be avoided. Use the Alignment attribute whenever possible.
	Clear	4.0+	4.0+	Determines whether an element can be displayed in line with a floating element.	
Position	Kind	4.0+	4.0+	Sets the origin position of a floating element.	
	Clipping	4.0+	4.0+	Crops the edges off a floating element.	Explorer 4.0 for the Mac does not properly display clipping. Item's positioning must be absolute for clipping to work.
	Z-Index	4.0+	4.0+	Controls the stacking order of floating elements.	
	Overflow	4.0+	4.0+	Controls what happens when an element's content exceeds its bounding box, such as getting cropped or being displayed with a scroll bar.	Navigator 4.0 does not recognize the Scroll attribute and has faulty support of the Hidden attribute.
	Visibility	4.0+	4.0+	Determines whether an element will be displayed.	
Border	Width	4.0+	4.0+	Controls the width of individual or all border lines.	
	Color	4.0+	4.0+	Controls the color of individual or all border lines.	
	Style	4.0+	4.0+	Controls the style of individual or all border lines.	Explorer 4.0 for Windows does not support dash or dot borders.
Background	Image	4.0+	4.0+	Specifies the background image.	
	Color	4.0+	4.0+	Specifies the background color.	
	Repeat	4.0+	4.0+	Controls whether the background image should be tiled.	
	Attach	4.0+	6.0+	Specifies whether background is fixed or scrolls with page.	
	Top	4.0+	6.0+	Sets the vertical position of a background image.	
	Left	4.0+	6.0+	Sets the horizontal position of a background image.	
List & Others	Image	4.0+	6.0+	Sets an image as a list marker.	
	Style	4.0+	4.0+	Sets a style for a list marker.	When setting an image as a list marker, set a style as a backup.
	Position	4.0+	6.0+	Specifies whether list item text wraps around the marker or is indented.	
	Other Property	—	—	Allows for the inclusion of CSS attributes not listed in GoLive, primarily for use with future additions to style sheets.	

Hex/RGB Conversion Chart

FFFFCC R=255 G=255 B=204	CC6600 R=204 G=102 B=000	CC3333 R=204 G=051 B=051	FF6699 R=255 G=102 B=153	CC6699 R=204 G=102 B=153	660066 R=102 G=000 B=102	9966CC R=153 G=102 B=204	660099 R=102 G=000 B=204	6666FF R=102 G=102 B=153	3333CC R=051 G=051 B=204
FFFF99 R=255 G=255 B=153	FF9966 R=255 G=153 B=102	CC0000 R=204 G=000 B=000	FF3399 R=255 G=051 B=153	CC3399 R=204 G=051 B=153	663366 R=102 G=051 B=102	9933FF R=153 G=051 B=255	663399 R=102 G=051 B=153	003366 R=000 G=051 B=153	3300FF R=051 G=000 B=255
FFFF66 R=255 G=255 B=102	FF6633 R=255 G=102 B=051	660000 R=102 G=000 B=000	FF0099 R=255 G=000 B=153	CC0099 R=204 G=000 B=153	990099 R=153 G=000 B=153	9900FF R=153 G=000 B=255	666699 R=102 G=102 B=153	333366 R=051 G=051 B=102	0000FF R=000 G=000 B=255
FFFF33 R=255 G=255 B=051	FF6600 R=255 G=102 B=000	990000 R=153 G=000 B=000	FF3366 R=255 G=051 B=102	FF66CC R=255 G=102 B=204	993399 R=153 G=051 B=153	9966FF R=153 G=102 B=255	9999CC R=153 G=153 B=204	000066 R=000 G=000 B=102	0033FF R=000 G=051 B=255
FFFF00 R=255 G=255 B=000	FF3300 R=255 G=051 B=000	993333 R=153 G=051 B=051	FF0066 R=255 G=000 B=102	FF33CC R=255 G=051 B=204	996699 R=153 G=102 B=153	CC00FF R=204 G=000 B=255	6666CC R=102 G=102 B=204	000099 R=000 G=000 B=153	3333FF R=051 G=051 B=255
FFCC33 R=255 G=204 B=051	CC3300 R=204 G=051 B=000	990033 R=153 G=000 B=051	CC3366 R=204 G=051 B=102	FF00CC R=255 G=000 B=204	CC00CC R=204 G=000 B=204	CC33FF R=204 G=051 B=255	6633CC R=102 G=051 B=204	330099 R=051 G=000 B=153	0066FF R=000 G=102 B=255
FFCC00 R=255 G=204 B=000	FF6666 R=255 G=102 B=102	996666 R=153 G=102 B=102	CC0066 R=204 G=000 B=102	FF33FF R=255 G=051 B=255	CC33CC R=204 G=051 B=204	CC66FF R=204 G=102 B=255	6600CC R=102 G=000 B=204	333399 R=051 G=051 B=153	3366FF R=051 G=102 B=255
FFCC99 R=255 G=204 B=153	FF3333 R=255 G=051 B=051	CC6666 R=204 G=102 B=102	993366 R=153 G=051 B=102	FF00FF R=255 G=000 B=255	CC66CC R=204 G=102 B=204	CC99FF R=204 G=153 B=255	9999FF R=153 G=153 B=255	003399 R=000 G=051 B=153	6699FF R=102 G=153 B=255
FFCC66 R=255 G=204 B=102	FF0033 R=255 G=000 B=051	CC9999 R=204 G=153 B=153	990066 R=153 G=000 B=102	FF66FF R=255 G=102 B=255	CC99CC R=204 G=153 B=204	000033 R=000 G=000 B=051	CCCCFF R=204 G=204 B=255	0000CC R=000 G=000 B=204	0099FF R=000 G=153 B=255
FF9900 R=255 G=153 B=000	FF0000 R=255 G=000 B=000	FF9999 R=255 G=153 B=153	660033 R=102 G=000 B=051	FF99FF R=255 G=153 B=255	9900CC R=153 G=000 B=204	330033 R=051 G=000 B=051	6600FF R=102 G=000 B=255	3300CC R=051 G=000 B=204	3399FF R=051 G=153 B=255
FF9933 R=255 G=153 B=051	CC0033 R=204 G=000 B=051	FFCCCC R=255 G=204 B=204	FF99CC R=255 G=153 B=204	FFCCFF R=255 G=204 B=255	9933CC R=153 G=051 B=204	330066 R=051 G=000 B=102	6633FF R=102 G=051 B=255	0033CC R=000 G=051 B=204	99CCFF R=153 G=204 B=255

RELATED TIPS:

Selecting and Replacing Colors, page 12
Expanding on the Web-safe Palette, page 16
Understanding Color Palettes, page 104

The chart below shows the 216 Web-safe colors with both their RGB and hexadecimal values specified. Note that while all of the numeric values are accurate, some of these colors fall outside of the CMYK spectrum rendered by the offset printing process. Therefore, the color swatches that appear here aren't necessarily representative of how they look onscreen.

Hexadecimal/RGB Value	
FF = 255	66 = 102
CC = 204	33 = 051
99 = 153	00 = 000

3366CC R=051 G=102 B=204	99FFFF R=153 G=255 B=255	336666 R=051 G=102 B=102	66CC99 R=102 G=204 B=153	66FF99 R=102 G=255 B=153	33CC66 R=051 G=204 B=102	66FF00 R=102 G=255 B=000	99CC66 R=153 G=204 B=102	666633 R=102 G=102 B=051	000000 R=000 G=000 B=000
0066CC R=000 G=102 B=204	33FFFF R=051 G=255 B=255	006666 R=000 G=102 B=102	33CC99 R=051 G=204 B=153	339900 R=051 G=153 B=000	00CC66 R=000 G=204 B=102	99FF33 R=153 G=255 B=051	99CC33 R=153 G=204 B=051	666600 R=102 G=102 B=000	333333 R=051 G=051 B=051
006699 R=000 G=102 B=153	66FFFF R=102 G=255 B=255	003333 R=000 G=051 B=051	00CC99 R=000 G=204 B=153	339933 R=051 G=153 B=051	66CC66 R=102 G=204 B=102	99FF00 R=153 G=255 B=000	99CC00 R=153 G=204 B=000	CC9966 R=204 G=153 B=102	666666 R=102 G=102 B=102
336699 R=051 G=102 B=153	00FFFF R=000 G=255 B=255	003300 R=000 G=051 B=000	00FFCC R=000 G=255 B=204	009933 R=000 G=153 B=051	00FF00 R=000 G=255 B=000	99FF66 R=153 G=255 B=102	99CC99 R=153 G=204 B=153	CC9933 R=204 G=153 B=051	999999 R=153 G=153 B=153
6699CC R=102 G=153 B=204	00CCCC R=000 G=204 B=204	333300 R=051 G=051 B=000	66FFCC R=102 G=255 B=204	009900 R=000 G=153 B=000	33FF33 R=051 G=255 B=051	CCFF00 R=204 G=255 B=000	CCCC99 R=204 G=204 B=153	CC9900 R=204 G=153 B=000	CCCCCC R=204 G=204 B=204
3399CC R=051 G=153 B=204	33CCCC R=051 G=204 B=204	336633 R=051 G=102 B=051	33FFCC R=051 G=255 B=204	66CC33 R=102 G=204 B=051	66FF66 R=102 G=255 B=102	CCFF33 R=204 G=255 B=051	CCCC66 R=204 G=204 B=102	993300 R=153 G=051 B=000	FFFFFF R=255 G=255 B=255
0099CC R=000 G=153 B=204	66CCCC R=102 G=204 B=204	336600 R=051 G=102 B=000	99FFCC R=153 G=255 B=204	66CC00 R=102 G=204 B=000	33FF66 R=051 G=255 B=102	CCFF66 R=204 G=255 B=102	CCCC00 R=204 G=204 B=000	996600 R=153 G=102 B=000	
00CCFF R=000 G=204 B=255	99CCCC R=153 G=204 B=204	006633 R=000 G=102 B=051	CCFFCC R=204 G=255 B=204	33CC00 R=051 G=204 B=000	00FF66 R=000 G=255 B=102	CCFF99 R=204 G=255 B=153	CCCC33 R=204 G=204 B=051	996633 R=153 G=102 B=051	
33CCFF R=051 G=204 B=255	009999 R=000 G=153 B=153	006600 R=000 G=102 B=000	99FF99 R=153 G=255 B=153	33CC33 R=051 G=204 B=051	00FF33 R=000 G=255 B=051	669966 R=102 G=153 B=102	999966 R=153 G=153 B=102	663300 R=102 G=051 B=000	
66CCFF R=102 G=204 B=255	339999 R=051 G=153 B=153	339966 R=051 G=153 B=102	33FF99 R=051 G=255 B=153	00CC33 R=000 G=204 B=051	33FF00 R=051 G=255 B=000	669900 R=102 G=153 B=000	999933 R=153 G=153 B=051	663333 R=102 G=051 B=051	
CCFFFF R=204 G=255 B=255	669999 R=102 G=153 B=153	009966 R=000 G=153 B=102	00FF99 R=000 G=255 B=153	00CC00 R=000 G=204 B=000	66FF33 R=102 G=255 B=051	669933 R=102 G=153 B=051	999900 R=153 G=153 B=000	330000 R=051 G=000 B=000	

Appendix

Glossary

a

alpha channel
An 8-bit grayscale selection that lets you manipulate, isolate, and protect a specific area of an image. See *mask*.

animated GIF
A GIF graphic file that includes multiple frames of motion that can be played back as an animation. See *GIF*.

anti-alias
A method of smoothing the jagged edges of type or line art on computer screens by adding pixels of intermediate color values along the object's edge.

artifacts
Wavelike patterns or blocky areas of banding that are sometimes created by JPEG compression.

attribute
A value in an HTML tag that specifies additional information about how the tagged element should be treated, such as height or color.

b

bitmap
A type of graphic file, most often used for continuous-tone photographic images, composed of an array of pixels. See *raster* and *vector graphic*.

browser
Software that communicates with Web servers and displays content on a computer screen. Netscape Navigator and Microsoft Internet Explorer are the two most common browsers.

c

Cascading Style Sheets
Sets of rules that can be applied to HTML documents and govern the placement, positioning, size, and other aspects of HTML text and graphical elements. See *style sheet*.

CGI
Common Gateway Interface. A set of rules that allows browsers and servers to exchange information based on requests from the browser.

CGI script
A program on a Web server that allows a browser to access another program on the server, such as a database. Can be used to process forms.

class
A group of HTML elements, selected by the designer, that can have the same layout attributes applied through a Cascading Style Sheet.

CMYK
The subtractive color model in which each pixel in the image contains a percentage value for the process inks used in printing: cyan, magenta, yellow, and black.

color reduction algorithm
The method of building a set, or palette, of colors for use in a GIF image and saving those color values in a table. Algorithms include perceptual, selective, adaptive, and Web. See *palette*.

color table
The values of all colors in a particular image file, used by image-editing software to convert between color models and by browsers to display images. Also called a color lookup table, CLUT, or color palette.

comment tag
Contains reference information in an HTML document that isn't displayed by a browser. See *metatag*.

common gateway interface
See *CGI*.

CSS
See *Cascading Style Sheets*.

d

DHTML
Dynamic HTML. A version of HTML that supports such technologies as Cascading Style Sheets and JavaScript, so pages can contain animation and interactivity.

dithering
A process of interpolating the values of adjacent pixels in an image to simulate intermediate colors and create smoother edges. The most common method applies an error-diffusion calculation.

dynamic HTML
See *DHTML*.

f

fill
A vector object's interior, to which a color or pattern can be applied. See *stroke*.

font
A complete set of uppercase and lower-case characters and punctuation marks in a typeface of a specific size, weight, and style.

frame
One image in a sequence of motion in a video, movie, or animation file.

frames
A feature of HTML that allows multiple documents to appear in separate areas of one browser window. The documents can interrelate but each can be updated and scrolled independently.

frameset
The HTML tag that defines the number and positioning of the frames that appear in a browser window.

g

GIF
Graphics Interchange Format. A bitmap file format that is widely used for the display of graphics on the Web. GIF files contain as many as 256 colors and support transparency and animation. See *animated GIF*, *JPEG*, and *PNG*.

h

head section
The part of an HTML document that contains information and tags about the page, such as its title and searchable keywords. The contents of the actual page are in the body section of the document.

hexadecimal
A base-16 numbering system used to define colors on the Web. It includes the digits 0 through 9 and the letters A through F (for 10 though 16). RGB colors expressed in hex triplets include three two-character pairs, such as #6A5ACD.

hotspot
An area of an image map defined by pixel coordinates that contains a link to another HTML document. See *image map*.

HTML
Hypertext Markup Language. Uses tags to define structural elements of documents published on the Web, including links to other documents.

hyperlink.
See *link*.

i

image map
An image used for navigation on the Web. Different areas of the image contain links to other HTML pages. See *hotspot*.

Internet
A decentralized, global computer network originally financed by the U.S. government to facilitate communication between academics and scientists.

j

JavaScript
A scripting language developed by Netscape allowing HTML authors to put interactivity and dynamic content— animation, sound, and rollover effects, for example—in their pages.

JPEG
A compressed bitmap file format designed for photographic images or images with many subtle color transitions. The name stands for Joint Photographic Experts Group, which developed the format for the International Standards Organization. See *GIF* and *PNG*.

k

keyframe
A specific moment in a timeline when an animated object's properties are defined. For example, keyframes denote the beginning and ending points of an object's transform or fade.

keyword
Describes the content of an HTML page and can be used by search engines to locate relevant documents.

l

link
Short for hyperlink. An element in an HTML document that lets the visitor click with the mouse to jump to another part of the document or to another page entirely.

loop
The number of times an animation or video file is played: once, a specific number of times, or forever.

lossy
Any compression scheme, such as that used with the JPEG format, that results in a loss of image data. Lossy compression can also be applied to GIF images to create smaller files at the expense of image quality.

m

mask
An isolated area of an image that is protected from color changes, filters, or other editing effects. A mask, which is an unselected area of an image, can be stored as an 8-bit grayscale channel. See *alpha channel*.

matte
A color, chosen to match a Web page background, that fills or blends with transparent pixels in an image that is placed over the background. Helps create a seamless edge between the image and the background.

metatag
A tag that includes information about the HTML document, such as keywords, that can be used by search engines. See *comment tag*.

n

navigational system
A graphical interface to a Web site that lets visitors find their way through contents and pages.

o

opacity
The degree of transparency of pixels in an image. See *transparency*.

optimize
To save graphic files for the Web with the most appropriate file format, and color palette and the smallest possible file size.

p

page
An HTML document containing text, images, and other elements.

palette
A set of colors than can be applied to GIF images for the Web. Commonly used palettes are adaptive, which is weighted toward the most commonly used colors in the image, and Web-safe, which includes only those colors common to both the Macintosh and Windows operating systems. See *color reduction algorithm*.

path
The outline of a vector shape.

PDF
Portable Document Format. An electronic file format developed by Adobe Systems based on a compressed form of PostScript. PDF files can be published to the Web and display documents with their original formatting intact.

pixel
Short for picture element. The smallest unit of measurement in a scanner or monitor.

PNG
A file format for graphic images supported by most, but not all, Web browsers. Comes in two forms: PNG-8, an alternative to GIF for graphic images and supports background transparency and matting; and PNG-24, an alternative to JPEG for photographic images that supports up to 256 levels of transparency. See *GIF* and *JPEG*.

r

raster See *bitmap*.

resolution
The degree of detail contained in a digital image, determined by the number of dots or pixels per inch. Images created for the Web are generally 72 pixels per inch.

RGB
The additive model used by computer monitors that blends red, green, and blue light to create a full spectrum of color.

rollover
An effect that can be triggered when a mouse cursor interacts with an HTML element. Effects are usually triggered by a mouse rolling over a specific area of an image and may include animation or sound. When an effect is applied to another area of the image, it is called a remote or secondary rollover.

s

search engine
Software that lets someone search for content on the Web or within a site using keywords.

site
A collection of related and linked Web pages with a cohesive navigational system that resides on one or more servers.

slice
A portion of an image cut to fit into an HTML table cell. Each slice of a large image can be optimized independently, contain a link, and support animation and rollover effects.

state
The image or file that appears in a browser before a rollover is triggered (the "off" state) or when it is activated (the "on" state).

stroke
A vector object's border, to which a weight, color, and/or pattern can be applied. See *fill*.

style sheet
A document that defines rules for the layout of an HTML file. The rules can be applied by style tags or style classes. See *Cascading Style Sheets*.

t

tables
A set of tags and attributes that allow HTML content to be displayed in cells, rows, and columns, giving greater control over the placement of elements on the page.

tags
Codes used to define content in an HTML document. A structural tag describes a document element, such as body text or an image; a style tag describes the layout.

tile
To arrange and repeat a graphic in an HTML page so that it appears as a single contiguous background image in a browser.

time delay
The time, in seconds, that elapses between the display of frames in an animation.

tolerance
The range from 0 to 255 that an image-editing tool uses when selecting or filling pixels. A low tolerance selects or fills pixels similar in color; a high tolerance selects or fills a broader range of colors.

transparency
Pixels with no color values, allowing a background color or pattern to show through. See *opacity*.

tween
To automatically create intermediate frames of motion in an animation. The term comes from *in betweening*, used in traditional animation.

U

URL
Uniform Resource Locator. The address of documents on the World Wide Web.

V

vector graphic
An image whose content is defined by lines and curves and measured by mathematical vectors. The alternative is bitmap. See *bitmap*.

W

Web-safe colors
A selection of 216 hues common to both the Mac and Windows operating systems that can be applied to GIF images to prevent dithering when the image is displayed in a browser on a 256-color monitor.

World Wide Web
The computers on the Internet that serve linked, formatted HTML documents. These documents can be accessed and viewed by any computer platform through a graphical browser.

Index

Contributors

Maria Giudice is founder and creative director of HOT Studio, Inc. (www.hotstudio.com), a San Francisco–based design agency committed to making information accessible and understandable across multiple media. With a design career spanning more than a decade, Maria is an established speaker, educatior, and author. *Web Design Essentials*, Second Edition, is Maria's fourth book on Web design and technology; she also coauthored the first edition of *Web Design Essentials,* as well as the award-winning first and second editions of *Elements of Web Design.* Maria teaches part-time at City College of San Francisco and lives in the East Bay with her husband, Scott Allen, and son, Max.

Anita Dennis is a freelance writer and editor in San Francisco who has covered electronic publishing, including both print and Web design as well as digital prepress, since 1993. A former executive editor at *Publish*, *MacWeek*, and *eMediaweekly*, her work has appeared in numerous technology and general interest publications, including *PC/Computing*, *Red Herring*, the *San Francisco Examiner*, and *Seybold Reports*. She writes a biweekly column about digital design and production issues for CreativePro.com, and she has written many features for Adobe.com. Anita has a master's in journalism from Columbia University.

Amy Franceschini founded Futurefarmers, a San Francisco–based multimedia design company, in 1995. Futurefarmers has an award-winning Web site (ww.futurefarmers.com) and has developed projects for a wide variety of clients, including Weiden & Kennedy (Nike), NEC, Autodesk, MSNBC, Dreamworks, and Levi Strauss. Amy also cofounded Atlas (www.atlasmagazine.com), an online magazine that was the first Web site to become part of the permanent collection of the San Francisco Museum of Modern Art.

We would also like to thank the following designers whose work appears in *Web Design Essentials, Second Edition*:

Renee Anderson: pages 12, 14, 40, 86

Zanne deJanvier: pages 20, 48, 50, 54, 92, 96

Jenny Eng: pages 38, 80, 112

Laura Dorothy Haertling: pages 98, 106, 108

Julia Hummelt: pages 16, 22, 36, 42, 46, 52, 62, 66, 68, 74, 82, 100

Dohyun Kim: pages 18, 32, 34, 72, 104

David Knupp: pages 20, 56, 58

Gregory Ramsperger: page 28

Noreen Santini: page 114

Susan E. Stanger: pages 10, 26, 78, 110

Michael H. Wong: page 80

Hot Studio, Inc.: pages 20, 34, 98